H.V. Morton's England

Merry Christmas
Francis
The Manor
1975

OVERLEAF Oast-houses in Kent
ENDPAPERS Norwich Cathedral

H. V. Morton's England

Eyre Methuen
London

First published in 1975
by Eyre Methuen Ltd
11 New Fetter Lane, London EC4P 4EE

Based on extracts taken from
In Search of England (Methuen 1927),
The Call of England (Methuen 1928) and
I Saw Two Englands (Methuen 1942).

Copyright © 1927, 1928; 1942,
and 1975 H.V.Morton

Edited by Patricia Haward
Designed by Tim Higgins

Printed and bound in Great Britain
by Hazell, Watson and Viney Limited
Aylesbury, Bucks

ISBN 0 413 31280 1

Contents

H. V. Morton's books on Britain

In Search of England   (1927)

The Call of England   (1928)

In Search of Scotland   (1929)

In Search of Ireland   (1930)

In Search of Wales   (1932)

In Scotland Again   (1933)

Ghosts of London   (1939)

H. V. Morton's London   (1940)
(a trilogy of earlier books)

I Saw Two Englands   (1942)

In Search of London   (1951)

Publisher's Foreword

H. V. MORTON's first travel books came out almost half a century ago. As a young reporter he drove his bullnosed Morris to the farthest corners of Britain and Ireland, following no special plan but returning with material for his 'Search' series. These famous books, starting with *In Search of England* in 1927, have never been out of print. In English alone their sales top one million. They appeal to readers of any age, who often retrace Morton's own journeys and write to tell him so.

The reason for this is simple. Travel writing at its best calls for imagination as much as for the writing skill to observe and report. Morton has imagination of two kinds. He can project himself back into history and capture distant events and the actors on stage at a particular place he visits. And when the people he meets are contemporaries, of the twentieth century, he understands them and their work with a sympathy they repay. This is just what we would like to manage on our own travels.

Here, embellished with new illustrations and maps, are selections from three famous books: *In Search of England*, *The Call of England*, and *I Saw Two Englands*. The photographs complement and add to H. V. Morton's text, emphasising that, for all Britain's surface changes, much of permanent value in the land he wrote about has survived for us and for our children.

It is intended to follow this selection with a second on the West of England and Wales; also with Scotland, Ireland, and London, each as one volume.

1 Kent

Not far from Maidstone, I found myself in a world of hops. They stretched in straight avenues on each side of the road. Here and there an oast-house lifted its tiled red cone above the trees, and with the freshness of the hedges and the tender green of the growing hops, formed a picture of Kent which I shall not easily forget.

I think hops are unquestionably the most picturesque crop we grow in this country. Though I prefer to look at a good field of ripe wheat or barley, for there is nothing lovelier than the corn-yellow of those crops and the sight of the wind moving them, there is something fascinating – almost exotic – about hops: they look as a vineyard ought to look.

In May there is a joyous, youthful eagerness in the way the green tendrils seem to race each other to the tops of the poles; later on, when the hops are ripe, the rustling, grasshopper-green tassels hang in graceful festoons, light as air against the darker background of their leaves.

Neither the vine nor the olive is as beautiful as the hop: and I have never seen on the Continent, or in the East, a vineyard or an olive-grove that could for a moment compare with the beauty of our Kentish hop-gardens.

Many of those who think of beer as our ancient national drink may be surprised to know that it was not originally an English drink at all. It was unknown in this country until the fifteenth century, and then it was detested as a nasty Dutch poison. 'It doth make a man fat,' wrote one critic, 'and doth inflate the belly, as it doth appear by the Dutche mens faces and belyes.'

Both hops and beer were imported from Holland and became popular with the Dutch community in London. Many towns in England tried to prevent the brewing of beer by forbidding the use of hops. Norwich did so in 1471, and in 1519 Shrewsbury prohibited

Hop picking

9

'This ancient road, perhaps the most ancient of all our roads, is believed to be haunted along certain of its stretches and, of course, if ever a road should be haunted it is the Pilgrims' Way.'

RIGHT Hops
BELOW Inside the
oast-house

the use of the 'wicked and pernicious weed – hops.' But beer gradually killed ale. In less than a hundred years beer was universally liked in England, and an observer of national customs could in 1577 even refer to ale, that grand old drink of his ancestors, as a thick, fulsome 'sick man's drink,' and popular no longer, except with a few old-fashioned die-hards.

IT WAS DELIGHTFUL to walk about Canterbury in the evening, with the sun still lighting the Cathedral towers and streets warm with life and bustle. The old houses and narrow lanes were pervaded by an air of ecclesiastical peace, plenty and privilege. Everyone I spoke to was distinguished by that smiling affability that comes so naturally to those who are always in brief contact with strangers.

Old streets, like Mercery Lane, cannot have changed much since the Middle Ages, either in appearance or in their function. They exist to sell cheap souvenirs which prove that the purchaser has been to Canterbury. These shops once sold leaden medallions of the head of St Thomas; now they sell postcards and ash-trays emblazoned with the city arms. I have the suspicion that an average band of Canterbury pilgrims were much the same a few centuries ago as those today who wander vaguely about the city on a day trip. Could you replace their curiosity with faith, or at least hope, I think you would have a similar crowd of people.

There was nothing wrong with pilgrimage except the pilgrim. In the East today you can still see medieval pilgrimage in being, and I have sometimes amused myself by picking out the characters of the *Canterbury Tales* from the motley throng that fills Jerusalem in Passion

LEFT Canterbury
Cathedral from the
Christchurch Gate
RIGHT Christchurch
Gate
BELOW Weaver's House,
Canterbury

Week. Still, when all is said and done, maybe one poor, simple-hearted creature with tears coursing down his cheeks, experiencing the bliss that neither wealth nor a science degree can give, cancels out all the hard-faced bargainers with God. And no doubt it was the same in Canterbury. In every pilgrimage there must have been at least one who redeemed the rest.

Soon after the cathedral was open in the morning, I went there and made the acquaintance of the Vesterer. I found him putting away the embroidered copes which had been used at the morning service. He had the keys of the safes with him, so I asked if I might see some of the treasures of Canterbury Cathedral.

The most beautiful object he showed me was a thin, hand-beaten chalice of silver-gilt which was discovered in the grave of a man who was buried in the year 1205. The man was Hubert Walter, Archbishop of Canterbury in the time of Richard Coeur de Lion. When his grave was opened in 1892, those who were present at the time looked with awe as they saw for one second, before the air caused the body to fall into dust, an archbishop vested, with his crozier beside him, just as he had been buried by the monks of Canterbury six hundred and eighty-seven years previously.

It is believed that Hubert Walter took the chalice with him to the Holy Land, when he went with Richard on the Third Crusade. If so, it was used at Mass long ago, among the palm trees at Acre. It does not often fall to any man's lot to hold a relic such as this.

Walter ruled England when the King was away. Among his constitutional innovations was the appointment of coroners. Few J.P.s know perhaps that they owe their office to him, for he appointed knights whose duty it was to enforce an oath to 'keep the peace', and such knights developed into our Justices of the Peace. When Richard died, Hubert Walter crowned John. He was the only person in England who could stand up to this King, and when he died John remarked: 'Now, for the first time am I truly King of England.'

The Vesterer offered to show me round the cathedral. We ascended spiral staircases to the triforium, then up again into the dark passages above the nave and transepts. It was like walking under the timbers of an old ship, dark and dusty, and with only an occasional handrail to guide one over the narrow planks which stretch across the vaulting. This is the exquisite roof which visitors admire from the floor of the church, but from this position it looks like a crop of enormous stone mushrooms growing in the darkness.

Perhaps few of those who admire the glory of Canterbury, of any other cathedral, know that between vaulting and roofing is this vast V-shaped no-man's-land where the wind whistles through slit

windows, where pigeons nest and where bats hang from rafters cut from oaks which were probably giants at the time of the Norman Conquest.

There was no beauty in this dim and unvisited region, but we explored it eagerly, discussing the marvels of thrust and counter-thrust, and admiring the workmen who made this stupendous church centuries ago.

We ascended the steps of the central tower, known as Bell Harry Tower, but before we had gone very far I was shown what must be one of the few medieval cranes in existence. It is a gigantic wheel, the size of a mill wheel, and was used by the masons of the Middle Ages

Vaulting in the Cathedral

17

to lift heavy stones from ground level to the summit of towers. It was worked by man-power. Several workmen stationed inside the wheel would walk, as if on a treadmill, which caused the wheel to revolve and wind up a rope to which stones were attached. It is still in perfect order, although I don't suppose it has been used for five centuries. Standing inside it, I discovered that the balance is so delicate that when I placed one foot only a few inches in advance of the other, the huge wheel began to revolve.

We climbed still higher – much higher – and came out on the summit of Bell Harry Tower. Below lay Canterbury in the calmness of a spring morning. The trees so far below hardly moved in the breeze, though a sharp wind was blowing across the tower. Looking down, the huge cruciform building is like a giant aeroplane, the transepts its wings, and the body of the church its fuselage.

CIVILISED ADULT HUMAN BEINGS are rarely in the habit of falling into ungovernable rages, of biting the carpet in fury and exhibiting other signs well known in badly conducted nurseries. But in early times our kings and nobles were not ashamed to give such violent exhibitions. They would roll on the floor, snapping at the rushes like dogs. They would scream. They would rave.

On a night towards the end of December, in the year 1170, King Henry II of England, who was then at the Castle of Bur, near Bayeux, fell into one of these royal rages. The cause of his anger was the action of Thomas à Becket, Archbishop of Canterbury, who for eighteen years had been fighting the State's attempt to dominate the Church.

Henry had forced Becket to be archbishop against his will, because he wished to have a complacent friend at the head of the Church he wished to attack. But he had chosen the wrong man. No sooner was Becket consecrated than he ceased to be the King's man and became God's man; and from that moment, and for eighteen years, the story of England is the fight between Church and State, between Becket and Henry.

On that night in December Henry worked himself into a frightful paroxysm. He called Becket 'a fellow that came to court on a lame horse with a cloak for a saddle'. He said that a man he had 'loaded with benefits' was insulting him. Then, turning to the assembled courtiers, he shouted: 'What sluggard wretches, what cowards have I brought up in my Court, who care nothing for their allegiance to their master! Not one will deliver me from this low-born priest!' He rushed from the hall.

That same night four men crossed the Channel: Reginald Fitzurse, William de Tracy, Richard le Breton, and Hugh de Moreville.

As I stood in the north transept of the cathedral, at the place where Becket died, I thought I would try to write a plain account of his murder, rejecting all fable and fancy and using only the facts supplied by men who saw it happen, or who were alive at the time.

The murder of the Archbishop is one of the best documented events in medieval history. He was slain in the Fleet Street of his time – if I may be forgiven the comparison – surrounded by the only reporters of that age, the monks and priests of the Church. Some who stood beside him, some who ran away and hid, others who vested his corpse for burial, have left descriptions from which it is possible to paint a true picture of that night eight hundred and more years ago.

In addition to many contemporary narratives, there are no fewer than five eye-witness accounts of Becket's death: the account of William of Canterbury, a monk; William Fitzstephen, a clerk in attendance on Becket; Benedict, another monk who was there; John of Salisbury; and Edward Grim, a clerk of Cambridge who was on a visit to Becket at the time. From these five accounts it is possible to reconstruct the murder in every detail; and this is what happened.

On the twenty-ninth of December, the day after the four knights had crossed the Channel, at three in the afternoon Becket sat down to dinner in the hall of the Archbishop's Palace, which was separated from the cathedral by the Great Cloister. He sat at the high table with his household and the monks, while at the long table sat the poor people and beggars whom he entertained every day.

At the end of dinner, after a thanksgiving had been sung, Becket went to his retiring-room, and the servants flung themselves on the broken meats. The sound was heard of horses clattering into the courtyard. In a few moments four knights in ordinary dress strode into the hall through the crowds of departing beggars.

The servants asked if the visitors would like something to eat, but they refused and went to Becket's room. The Archbishop, seated on a couch, was leaning on the shoulder of a monk, while monks reclined on the floor near him. He was over six feet in height, handsome, and with a keen and piercing eye. He was fifty-two years of age and, though his figure was really spare, he felt the cold so acutely that he wore an incredible number of garments in order to keep warm; and these gave him a padded, corpulent appearance.

As the knights entered, he continued to talk with the monk next to him. They came in silently, without a greeting, and sat on the floor at his feet. Then Becket looked at them and spoke to Tracy by name. The knights began to talk violently.

They charged Becket with undermining the royal authority and with causing disturbances, and they demanded that he should lift the ban of excommunication from the Bishops of London and Salisbury. Becket, who was a man of quick temper, also raised his voice, and soon knights and Archbishop were quarrelling violently.

The knights flew into one of their Norman passions and stamped about the room, twisting their long gauntlets, advancing close to Becket, gnashing their teeth and waving their arms. They screamed that he had threatened to excommunicate them; he shouted back that they could not frighten him.

'Were all the swords in England hanging over my head,' he shouted, 'you could not terrify me from my obedience to God, and my lord the Pope.'

Crowds of monks and servants ran into the room and gathered round Becket. The knights roared at them to stand back if they were loyal to the King. They refused to move. The room was soon a pandemonium, and through it the knights ran to the door shouting, 'To arms, to arms!'

It was now nearly five o'clock. The winter's darkness had fallen. Beneath a sycamore tree in the courtyard the knights put on their armour. The monks bolted the doors and Becket sat down again on his couch. Some of the monks, discussing the scene, believed there was nothing to fear because, as William Fitzstephen noted, 'the men had come drunk' and 'would not have spoken like that before dinner'. Others were not so sanguine. At this moment a frightened monk rushed in to say the knights were arming. All save a few companions fled into the cathedral. 'All monks are cowards,' said Becket. His attendants, believing that the knights would not dare to shed blood on consecrated ground, forced Becket against his will to leave the palace. Half pushed, half lifted, he was taken through the cloisters and into the dark church, where vespers had just begun. As they gained what some hoped was sanctuary, they heard behind them the crash of woodwork as the knights broke into the palace.

What then happened took place in almost complete darkness, a darkness lit only by tapers burning before the shrines. A hammering echoed through the church. Becket ordered the doors to be opened, and when no one would do it, he strode forward and himself flung back the bars. A terrified crowd of monks fought to enter. Becket helped them, saying, 'Come in, come in, faster, faster!'

By this time the church was full of flying and hiding men. Only three remained with the Archbishop: Robert of Merton, William Fitzstephen, his chaplain, and Edward Grim, the clerk. They tried to get Becket to hide in the crypt or in the triforium, where he would never have been discovered, but he declined to do so. At last they persuaded him to mount the steps from the north transept, in which they were standing, to the choir but, as they did so, the knights,

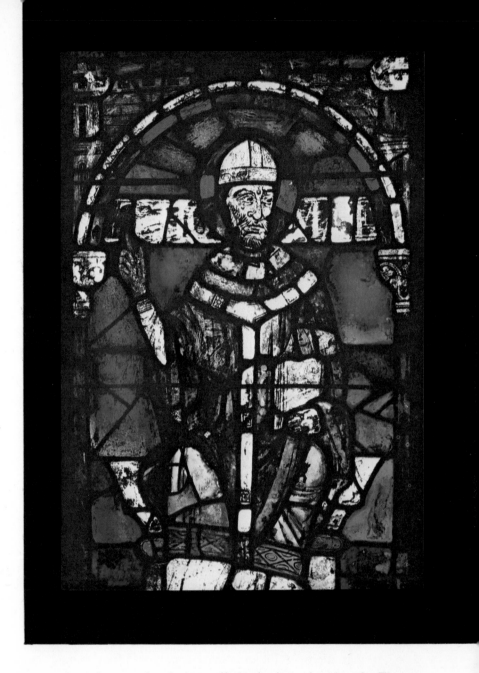

Window, Chapel of
St Thomas

covered to the eyes in chain mail, broke into the church. Fitzurse
came first, with a sword in one hand and a carpenter's axe, which he
had picked up in the palace, in the other. He could see nothing in
the darkness and stood calling for the 'traitor Becket'. There was
silence. He called again, and then Becket came down the steps.

'Reginald, why do you come into my church armed?' he asked.

Fitzurse placed the carpenter's axe against Becket's chest and said:
'You shall die. I will tear out your heart!'

St Augustine's Chair

'I am ready to die,' replied Becket, 'for God and the Church, but I warn you, I curse you in the name of God Almighty, if you do not let my men escape.'

The knights, fearing to commit sacrilege, then tried to hustle Becket out of the church. 'I will not fly, you detestable fellow!' he shouted, pushing Fitzurse away. Then they tried to place him on Tracy's shoulders, but Becket seized Tracy and flung him to the floor. At that moment Fitzurse came up with lifted sword, and Becket, now furious, cried out, 'You profligate wretch, you are my man – you have done me fealty – you ought not to touch me!'

Fitzurse shouted back: 'I owe you no fealty or homage contrary to my fealty to the King,' and made a blow at Becket's head. It did not touch him, but knocked back his skull cap.

Tracy then came up and aimed a blow which the clerk, Grim, who had his arm round Becket, tried to parry. The blow cut Grim's arm and grazed the crown of Becket's head, and also cut into his shoulder.

'For the name of Jesus, and the defence of the Church, I am ready to die,' whispered Becket and, with those words, fell flat on his face. Richard le Breton stood over him and delivered a tremendous blow which severed the top of the skull; so violent a blow that the sword snapped as it met the marble floor.

Hugh of Horsea, a sub-deacon who had joined the murderers, was then taunted with having taken no part in the murder. He came up and thrust his sword into the wound, scattering Becket's brains over the pavement.

So, with Becket newly slain on the floor of his church, the murderers, beside themselves with rage and triumph, ran through the cloisters, shouting 'The King's men, the King's men!' as if they had been in battle, for that was the warcry of the English; and as they rode away, a thunderstorm of great violence broke over Canterbury, striking terror into the hearts of the people.

That night a strange scene took place before the high altar. The monks undressed the body of Becket for burial. They took off the incredible assortment of garments which covered him. First a brown mantle, then a white surplice, then a long coat of lamb's wool, then two woollen pelisses, then – to their utter astonishment – the black robe of a Benedictine monk. At the sight of it their grief and emotion knew no bounds. It astounded them to think that the Archbishop, whom they had regarded as a great noble, fond of purple and fine linen, should have secretly assumed a monk's habit.

A greater surprise awaited them. When they stripped the body, they saw that Becket wore a hair shirt next to his skin and that beneath it his body was marked with the weals of scourging. So he was a more austere monk than any of them!

Then they saw a thing which is nauseating to our minds today, but in those days proved beyond doubt that a man had subdued the flesh and humiliated the body in order that his soul might shine; they saw that Becket's hair shirt crawled with vermin. Their joy and amazement at this revolting sight were boundless, and they cried, as indeed I can imagine a Coptic monk of Egypt crying today: 'He was one of God's saints!'

So on the very night he died, within a few hours of his martyrdom, Thomas à Becket was hailed as St Thomas of Canterbury.

I ARRIVED AT WALMER, the residence of the Lord Warden of the Cinque Ports, on one of the days when it was open to the public. I should have been happy to while away the time in the garden, enjoying the scent of the flowers and the hum of the bees, but I felt that I ought to know something about the rooms in which the Iron Duke laid down his eighty-three years.

As soon as I entered the room where the Duke of Wellington died, it captured me completely. Its sternness, its simplicity, its touch of almost priggish discomfort, and its lonely pathos, seemed to reflect the life that had been lived there. It has been kept, whether by accident or design I do not know, almost exactly as it was the day he died. Nothing has been altered. You almost expect the door to open and to see the old Duke, hook-nosed and silver-haired, glide in with a frosty gleam of blue eyes.

Wellington made no concessions to old age. With the whole of Walmer Castle to live in, he preferred one small bed-sitting room modelled on the tent of a subaltern; and a frugal subaltern at that. His bed was an iron camp bed three feet wide. He allowed himself no luxurious blankets, but only a German quilt. The one sybaritic touch is a horse-hair pillow covered with chamois leather, and this he used to take about with him whenever he spent a night away.

A mahogany desk, a few books, a few engravings, a reading-desk, at which he wrote his letters standing, and one or two chairs, complete the furniture. An ivory statuette of Napoleon sitting astride a chair used to stand on the mantelpiece.

This grand old Tory, who resisted every reform with the stern formality of his native century, the eighteenth, remained a national hero all his later life, with one brief exception. When he opposed the Reform Bill, he rode slowly through London, high-nosed and bleak, to the jeers of a mob and to a hail of brickbats and mud. As he reached Apsley House in Piccadilly, he turned and said to the police-constable by his side: 'An odd day for them to choose.' He had remembered that it was the anniversary of Waterloo.

As he grew older, his role merged naturally from that of Achilles into that of Nestor. They consulted him about everything. When the Crystal Palace was first erected in Hyde Park, the London sparrows failed to show proper respect for the assembled works of art, and with so much glass about, it was impossible to shoot them. So the Queen sent for the Duke: the dear Duke would know what to do.

'Try sparrow hawks, Ma'am,' he said instantly.

'It was Wellington's last victory,' commented Mr Philip Guedalla, in *The Duke*.

Perhaps his last victory was the conquest of age. At eighty he was as bright and sprightly as a robin. To the public, he was always a tight-buttoned, reserved figure, aloof from the warmer passions of life, and great would have been the astonishment could the public have seen the Duke now and then behind the ramparts of Walmer.

He loved children to stay with him. Before dinner he would dress, always in the uniform of Lord Warden, a blue coat with red facings and tight, white overalls strapped under the boot, and would sit

reading the newspaper. The children then played a game which they called 'the Battle of Waterloo'. This began when one of them threw a cushion at the Duke's paper.

Walmer Castle

Lord Stanhope, in his *Notes of Conversations with the Duke of Wellington*, tells how on one occasion the old man learned that the small children of Lord and Lady Robert Grosvenor, who were staying with him, loved to receive letters by post. Every day he took the trouble to write to each of them a careful little letter which was posted and delivered by a Castle servant.

He was fond of filling his pockets with surprises, and it is recorded that on one almost unbelievable occasion he appeared to the children who were staying at the Castle dressed up like a Christmas tree, with toys tied all over him! No one living at the time would have believed this, for in public he never permitted one hint of human feeling to escape him. He was an icy, forbidding old man, high-handed, formal, and bitingly candid in his comments about men and affairs.

He died in the little bastion room after only a few hours' illness. He was buried to the sound of a nation's grief, and when the guns boomed across London as his funeral car swayed through the hushed streets to St Paul's, England said farewell to the eighteenth century.

25

The Westerham statue
of Wolfe

WESTERHAM WEARS AN AIR of age and quality. I have no doubt that the people who live there are agreeable, sensible folk. It must be admitted, however, that they have ruined the approach to their town on one side by permitting a rash of villas to be built there, but they must at least be congratulated that this lapse in architectural manners cannot be seen from the harmonious main street.

On the town green, which slopes gracefully downhill, I saw the statue of a man waving a sword. He wears a long-waisted coat to his knees, a peruke and a tricorn hat. It is a good statue and an excellent likeness. Wolfe's sharp, rather peaky features have been admirably portrayed, and although there is nothing dramatic in the way he lifts his sword, there is a dramatic appeal in the isolation of his graceful figure against the sky of his native town. He stands there, it seems, not in the centre of a Kentish market town, but high upon the far-off Plains of Abraham.

Unlike prophets, soldiers are rarely forgotten in their own country towns, partly perhaps because they offer the sculptor some scope for effect. And certainly Wolfe has not been forgotten in Westerham. His figure is the most prominent object in the town.

I thought I would go and look at the house, now called Quebec House, where Wolfe lived when he was a boy. It stands a few yards out of the town, at the bottom of the hilly road leading to Sevenoaks, a dignified mansion of Kent brick, with three gables and three storeys.

Wolfe was not born in this house, but in the vicarage which his father, a colonel in the Army, had rented from the vicar. The family moved into Quebec House when Wolfe was an infant and they remained there for about ten years.

I was shown into a panelled hall and into a panelled room to the right, which was full of relics. It is difficult to say what degree of fame must be achieved by a hero before such objects as 'eight table knives, eight table forks and one carving fork, formerly in the possession of the Wolfe family' cease to be ridiculous when placed in a glass case. But hero-worship is a profound and deep-seated emotion, and it is undoubtedly true that many people who have no interest in Wolfe, and could give you no clear idea of his life and achievements, have probably gazed with reverence at those knives and forks.

How extraordinarily alike were Wolfe and Nelson, both frail and delicate children and never robust as men, both of them nervous, quick, emotional and talkative, possessing too that rare quality which caused them to be worshipped by the common soldiers and sailors who served under them, and, at the last, meeting the two most dramatic deaths in British history, expiring in the moment of their triumph as if upon a stage.

26

Perhaps they were both throw-backs to an earlier England, maybe to the emotional Tudor England when men boasted and bragged and were unashamed to shed a tear. Already in their time the upper-class Englishman was, I suspect, altering. He was already on his way to the public school. And it is interesting to remember that upon two notable occasions both Wolfe and Nelson were considered by certain of their contemporaries to have behaved in a manner not befitting the dignity of gentlemen. Before Wolfe sailed for America he dined with Pitt and Temple, and it is said that after dinner, worked up by the thought of the great mission that lay before him, he drew his sword and, to the embarrassment of his hosts, burst 'into a storm of gasconade and bravado' which shocked them profoundly. But I am willing to wager that neither Shakespeare, Drake nor Raleigh would have been shocked or embarrassed by such behaviour. Nelson had precisely the same effect on the Duke of Wellington upon the only occasion those two great men met. It was in the waiting-room of the old Colonial Office in Downing Street. The Duke entered the room and saw a little man with one arm waiting there. He recognised Nelson. As the Duke himself described this meeting, Nelson 'entered at once into conversation with me, if I can call it conversation, for it was almost all on his side and all about himself, and in, really, a style so vain and so silly as to surprise and almost disgust me'. No doubt the Duke would have been equally disgusted with any of the other Elizabethans.

It would indeed be interesting to know the precise period in history when it became ungentlemanly for Englishmen to cry in public, or to boast or brag and indulge in picturesque rhetoric; in other words, the precise moment when the strong, silent, public-school Englishman became the masculine pattern of English conduct.

WHEN I WAS TRAVELLING IN SYRIA some years ago I became interested in the life of that extraordinary woman, Lady Hester Stanhope, a niece of the great Lord Chatham, who cut her-self off from England and went to live in barbaric state in the hills of the Lebanon, above Beirut.

Every traveller of note who went to Syria in the nineteenth century sought an audience with her, which was not always granted; and nearly every book of travel or reminiscences written at that time gives an account of her strange receptions, her Eastern dress, her pipe-smoking, her Arab guards, her belief in magic and prophecy, and her exhausting harangues to those who had penetrated her mountain fastness.

The ancestral home of the Stanhopes is at Chevening Place, in Kent, a few miles north-west of Sevenoaks. At this point the old

Pilgrim's Way from Winchester to Canterbury drops down from Surrey into Kent, and until 1792 the road used to run through Chevening Park.*

The house, which stands in a splendid park, is a good example of those formal town houses which Inigo Jones and his contemporaries planted so uncompromisingly amid the green meadows and the woodlands of England. It remains today much as it left the restless hands of the third earl, who, to the dismay of his descendants, covered the fine red brick with cream-coloured tiles, thus ruining the exterior. It is a tall, disguised Stuart house, with two curving wings on each side, enclosing a wide entrance courtyard separated from the park by iron railings. It is a house that seems still to live in the atmosphere of four-horse coaches and I felt that a motor car looked rather ill at ease in the courtyard.

KNOLE HOUSE STANDS a little way out of Sevenoaks in a fine park full of ancient trees, oak, beech and sycamore. Herds of deer stand beneath the trees, and the more adventurous occasionally advance into the open to accept or reject a biscuit offered by some lover of animals.

I drove in through the gates and saw the house far off looking as though several colleges in Oxford or Cambridge were taking a walk together in the country. The place, enormous as it looks from a distance, seems to grow larger as you approach it, and I had the uneasy feeling, as I saw the hundreds of windows, that crowds of people, invisible to me, must be watching my solitary advance. But when I reached the noble and austere west front, with its five gables on each side of a grey, embattled gatehouse, there was not a soul to be seen.

When Richard Sackville, the 3rd Earl of Dorset, inherited Knole in 1609, one hundred and twenty-six people sat down to meals in the house every day: steward, chaplain, clerks, cooks, yeomen of the pantry and the buttery, slaughtermen, brewer and under-brewer, footmen, servants, falconer, armourer, grooms, stablemen, and all the other inhabitants of a self-contained community. Today Lord Sackville, the descendant of a family which has inhabited Knole for over three centuries, occupies only a corner of the immense place.

The visitor to Knole finds himself in a maze of corridors and apartments rather like the oldest part of Rome. The long, narrow streets, which are corridors, open out into a piazza, which is a room, and then with haphazard irregularity branch off again to others.

---

* The house has since been given to the nation by Lord Stanhope and is now the official residence of Prince Charles.

28

The main impression is of tall windows full of diamond glass, sunlight burning through stained-glass armorial shields, of hundreds of fine pictures of sad men and women, oak chairs, walnut chairs, and mahogany chairs; and of velvets, brocades and tapestries worn and mellowed by Time.

It is hardly possible that the whole of Knole could ever have been inhabited at one time. There must always have been large uninhabited areas. Even Jacobean Sackvilles must have said to their wives: 'We must make up our minds to go over and live in the east wing next year.' Miss Victoria Sackville-West confessed that 'after a life-time of familiarity, I still catch myself pausing to think of the shortest route from one room to another'.

Knole,
the south front

29

2 Sussex and Hampshire

'WHY IS IT THAT THE OXEN, the swine, the women, and all other animals, are so long-legged in Sussex?' asked John Burton in 1771. 'May it be from the difficulty of pulling the feet out of so much mud by the strength of the ankles that the muscles get stretched, as it were, and the bones lengthened?'

The worker in the Wealden clay still knows that 'Sowsexe is full of dyrt and myre,' and to our ancestors that was the distinguishing feature of the county.

Until almost modern times the roads in Sussex were so unspeakably bad that judges on circuit rarely ventured beyond the border towns of Horsham and East Grinstead, and when Defoe was in Sussex only a little over two hundred years ago, he saw a lady of 'very good quality' going to church in a coach drawn by six oxen. He also noted that felled trees sometimes lay for a year, until the muddy roads were dry enough for them to be dragged away by ox teams.

It was undoubtedly the horror which the roads of Sussex inspired in the minds of our ancestors which enabled the county to keep to itself, and retain that rich dialect and mass of local custom and superstition which delighted the people who wrote about Sussex even as recently as the end of last century.

Since that time Sussex has suffered an invasion almost as complete and overwhelming as that which transformed the northern towns during the first stage of the Industrial Revolution. But the Sussex invasion was not of workers, but of retired people and wealthy weekenders. The Sussex squire has been replaced by the London stockjobber, and the Sussex cottage has become the paradise of the London financier. It is interesting to notice, as you motor through Sussex today, that while the old squire, like Charles II, took a long time in dying, the new squires are dying by the score, as the 'To Be Sold' boards outside so many large houses clearly indicate.

The Sussex coast probably contains more thriving and populous

A Sussex lane

31

towns than any similar coastal area in England. They lie in a long chain: Hastings, St Leonards, Eastbourne, Brighton, Worthing, Littlehampton and Bognor Regis. Some of the settlements on the Sussex coast are among the most hideous objects in modern England. They have been run up by speculative builders and amateur builders, and have ruined large parts of what was once a superb stretch of coast. The only consolation is that already they seem to be falling down.

Towns like Eastbourne and Brighton should increase in dignity with the years, if local authorities will keep a keen watch on architects. Eastbourne is pleasantly Edwardian, and Brighton is, with the exception of Regent's Park in London, the most perfect example of the Regency period in England. But already in Brighton the rot is setting in; and if it goes on, no one with any taste will ever go there.

The Sussex invasion still continues, and is having its effect on that older agricultural Sussex which carries on unobtrusively in the small towns and villages. The famous Southdown sheep are being driven off the Downs, for the growth of the huge seaside towns has created a tremendous demand for milk, with the result that cows are now becoming more profitable than sheep.

IF TOWNS LIVED UP TO THEIR NAMES, Battle would be a place where men went red in the face with rage, gnashing their teeth and pushing people off the pavement. But in reality it is one of the drowsiest and most peaceful little towns in Sussex. It has its share of the cafés and antique shops which establish themselves in all places where visitors assemble, and the only danger likely to be encountered in Battle today is the prices of antiques.

Only in England perhaps could Battle Abbey become a girls' school. Indeed it might seem to a foreigner to be one of the baffling

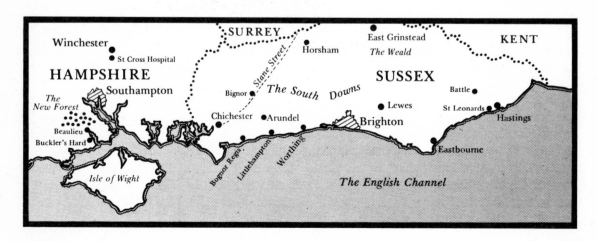

Battle Abbey

inconsistencies of English life that the place where the future of England was changed should be devoted to the education of young ladies; for here, if anywhere, is a sacred national shrine.

Every schoolboy knows that Battle Abbey was built by William the Conquerer in fulfilment of a vow made before the battle of Hastings. He did not like the look of the Saxon army. In spite of the fact that it had been drinking and making merry the night before, it had a tough appearance as it stood on the well-chosen hill, and the Conqueror vowed that should victory be granted to him, he would endow an abbey on the battlefield.

The abbey he built was a tremendous place about a mile in area and endowed with lands stretching for three miles round its walls. The abbot had a seat in Parliament, and among the abbey's

33

On top of the Downs

privileges was the right to give sanctuary to all unhappy wretches and fugitives from justice who gained the safety of its doors.

The Abbey was pulled down by the orders of Henry VIII, but the foundations still remain and it is possible to see where the altar stood and where the apse of the church ended. It is recorded that William chose for the high altar the exact place where Harold fell.

I should like to see a notice here telling people that they are standing on the place where the Saxon army camped on an unlucky day, Friday, the 13th of October, in 1066. There were about twelve thousand of them, mostly rough countrymen, badly armed and ill disciplined, slovenly, careless, but without fear. It is said that they drank and danced around their fires all night, crying 'bublie' and 'wassail', 'laticome' and 'drinkhail', while in the opposing camp the Norman army confessed to its sins and attended Mass.

William's army was not much greater in numbers than Harold's, but it was infinitely superior in its weapons and theory of warfare. It was completely up-to-date. Even cross-bows, which had just been invented, had a place in it. Most important of all, the Norman cavalry was the last word in shock tactics.

If you walk down from the place of the high altar and come to the terrace, you will see a few fields, some cows grazing, and trees, a quiet English scene. It was across those fields that the Normans charged to victory, and it seems strange that the destiny of England could have been settled in a few small meadows. What a noise the Battle of Hastings has made in the world, yet what a minor brawl it was! What minor brawls all wars were in ancient times: a few men trying to kill each other in a meadow. It is only today, when Man calls himself civilised, that whole nations go to war, and even include their women and children in it.

IN QUIET LANES about three miles south of Fittleworth, a cottage stands by itself near the village of Bignor. I knocked at the door and asked if I could see the Roman villa.

A pleasant smiling woman gave me a ticket and removed a bunch of keys from a hook; and we crossed the lane and mounted a rising path that ran on the edge of a wheat-field. When we had walked a hundred yards or so, the woman turned round and pointed with the keys towards the way we had come. The landscape is dominated by the South Downs, whose smooth northern slopes descend in gentle sweeps to the fields and the meadows of the Rother Valley.

'There's Stane Street,' she said. 'Can you see it coming down towards us?'

And I saw, like a straight line drawn in apple green upon the darker emerald of the Downs, the ghost of the great Roman road that

once joined Regnum, which is now Chichester, with a port on the Thames called Londinium. We turned and went on beside the field of wheat.

Bignor, site of the Roman villa

The Roman villa we were approaching was discovered by a ploughman in the year 1811. His ploughshare struck something large and hard, which turned out to be a coloured pavement. As he scraped away the soil, Ganymede, borne godwards in an eagle's claws, looked at him out of the Sussex mire; being a Saxon, the man did not recognise him and ran off to ask Mr Tupper, the farmer, to come and have a look. Then came the discovery of more coloured pavements, of dining rooms and reception rooms, centrally heated, of baths, bedrooms, barns, stables and outhouses. It was one of the three finest Roman villas in England; as fine as the Woodchester villa in Gloucestershire, and the villa at Brading, in the Isle of Wight. Experts think it was built about AD 79, the year the Emperor Vespasian died.

We went round unlocking doors and unpadlocking wooden shutters, and through each opened door and shutter shot a beam of light which streamed down on the coloured mosaic pavements. The pavements of seven rooms have been preserved in a fragmentary condition, but all the fragments are large enough to give a good idea of the complete design.

37

It was interesting to see patterns which I have seen in Pompeii and Herculaneum, and in more remote places of the Roman Empire, lying in a Sussex meadow. One pattern seems to have been a monotonously popular one with Roman artists. It must have occupied the place in Roman interior decoration that 'The Monarch of the Glen' occupied in Victorian dining-rooms. This is 'The Four Seasons', a geometrical design with allegorical heads in the four corners, representing the Seasons of the Year.

A fine head of Winter is to be seen at Bignor, a human face in a hooded cloak, wearing an expression of gloomy hopelessness, as if asking: 'Is this weather *ever* going to improve?' The finest pavement shows a stately head, probably of Juno, flanked by peacocks, an emblem of immortality. Below the usual geometrical borders is an interesting strip which shows twelve cupids playing at gladiators.

'Can you imagine what England was like when people lived in this house?' I asked the woman.

Mosaic: Head of Winter

'Well, they knew how to make themselves comfortable,' she replied, like a practical housewife, 'with their central heating and swimming-pools and such like.'

No doubt they did, but I imagine that comfort was unevenly distributed. I think if I could make a brief exploration into the past I should choose to travel for a week or so through Hadrian's Britain. I should give much to see what London was like, what a country town such as Silchester or Chichester was like, and what a British village was like. It would be interesting to see where Romanisation ended, and to know if the peasants bore any ill feeling towards the upper-class Romanised Celts. I should expect to find wealthy landowners, townsmen and shop-keepers priding themselves on their Roman habits and fashions, assembling in the forum, going to the theatre, even maybe trying hopelessly to cultivate the olive and the grape; but I should expect to find the British villagers still primitive and Celtic-speaking and looked down upon, possibly with a touch of patronising affection, by the Romanised Britons of the towns. Perhaps some young upper-class Briton in a toga might be seen exploring the villages with the object of studying the folklore of his countrymen, and of copying down for the delight of a sophisticated public the simple stories told round wood fires in stockaded encampments.

THE FITZALAN CHAPEL at Arundel is the burial-place of the Earls of Arundel and Dukes of Norfolk. It is one of the most wonderful tomb chapels in England, a place that, though it was badly knocked about during the Civil War, is still the loveliest thing to see in Arundel. I know few burial-places in which the fear of death seems less present.

The nobles of Arundel, separated by many centuries and ending with the late Duke of Norfolk, lie, their feet to the altar, resting on the FitzAlan horse; their heads are on marble cushions and their hands are clasped in prayer. The South Chantry, which was built about 1498, is one of the most beautiful tombs in England. Petworth marble has been carved to resemble the finest lace.

In the centre of the chapel, surrounded by a screen of medieval iron work, lie Thomas FitzAlan and his Countess, the daughter of John, King of Portugal. They died in the fifteenth century. She is sculptured in her best clothes, a horned headdress on her head, a gown sewn with pearls, the tight sleeves seamed with pearls. The guide told me that when a Requiem Mass is celebrated, ten candles of unbleached wax are burned on the ten prickets of the screen which surrounds their tomb.

Nearby is the grave of John FitzAlan, who lost a leg and died at the siege of Beauvais in 1435. For centuries there was a mystery about his body. It was brought home by a man called Elton, who demanded 1,400 marks, which the family refused to pay. Elton therefore kept the body in pawn for a number of years, and it was not definitely known to have been redeemed and buried in the family vault until 1859, when the tomb was opened and the bystanders saw the old warrior lying there with only one leg.

OLD WILLIAM CAMDEN, writing about Chichester, said: 'The city hath four gates, opening to *the four quarters of the world.*' I like that fine flourish, which seems to link the homely outskirts of Chichester with Trebizond and Samarkand.

Although the four gates have gone, the four main streets of Chichester are called North, South, East and West Streets, and you will not find a better example in England of a city that was planned eighteen centuries ago by the legions of Rome.

The American grid-iron cities were, of course, the rule in the Ancient World. No Greek or Roman would have been surprised by New York. Alexander the Great built Alexandria three hundred years before Christ just as a modern American architect would do: and all the Hellenistic cities of the period were designed on the rectangular principle.

When, therefore, did the winding street and the narrow alley begin? I remember once sitting among the ruins of Ephesus, looking at the marble bones of the old city, which lie under the grass and the shrubs. Shepherd-boys were wandering through the ruins with their goats, and I noticed that, as the animals wandered here and there in search of grass and herbage, they trod winding paths which cut across the plan of the city. I have an idea that goats and sheep are the architects of the medieval lane!

If there is anything in this theory, cities like Chichester can never have been entirely ruined or deserted, because their Roman street plan is too perfect. Either citizens with a Roman municipal education survived to carry on through the Dark Ages, or the Saxons conquered their dislike of a town wall and consented to live within it.

As soon as I entered Chichester, I felt it to be a comfortable and friendly place, which I should like to visit again and for a longer time. So far as physical appearances go, it would seem to have a greater affinity with Gloucester than with any town in Sussex; although I had only to listen to the people who crowded the narrow pavements to realise that Chichester is to West Sussex as Lewes is to East Sussex.

Let us hope that nothing will ever persuade Chichester to remove its wonderful Market Cross, the best in England, planted in the very heart of the city, where the four points of the compass meet.

Arundel Castle

It stands in what was once the middle of Roman Regnum, the beginning of that North Street which, as soon as it left the gate of Regnum became the famous Stane Street that flew to London over Down and across Weald, as the crow flies. It reached London Bridge, a little over fifty-five miles away, with a divergence of only about a mile and a half. What a marvellous engineering feat this was.

The dignity and pride of Chichester resides in its cathedral, a huge mass of worn, elephant-coloured stone lifting itself from grass on the side of West Street. It has one unique feature: the only detached cathedral belfry in England, a tall fifteenth-century tower in the north-west corner of the churchyard, which visitors may enter and ascend. Suspended in the darkness there you see 'Big Walter', the hour bell, which weighs 74 hundredweight, and a peal of bells of various ages, the oldest bearing the date 1583.

As soon as I entered the beautifully kept cathedral, I was impressed by its extraordinary width. The nave is nineteen feet wider

LEFT Chichester's market cross

ABOVE The Bar Gate, Southampton

'I stood on the Bar Gate at
Southampton and looked down over
the town of Sir Bevis. In the air
was the nearness of great ships.'

Chichester Cathedral

than those of Westminster Abbey and Canterbury Cathedral, and with the exception of St Paul's and York Minster it is the widest cathedral nave in the country. This peculiarity is caused by double aisles. I have seen these only in old churches which have been enlarged to accommodate an expanding parish.

How exquisite is the calm dignity of the architecture, chiefly Norman, of this church, and how fortunate it is that no one has blocked the view with a hideous organ; you can see straight down the church from the west door to the east window.

Behind the high altar I saw the place where the shrine of St Richard of Chichester used to stand, at one time a great place of pilgrimage, as famous, almost, as the shrine of Thomas of Canterbury. An inscription in the retro-choir says that St Richard's body was moved there from the nave on 16 June, 1276, in the presence of King Edward I and the chief people of the realm.

44

Richard's life is proof that violence and murder print a name on the future more securely than goodness and sanctity. Most people can tell you something about Thomas à Becket, but few could describe the life of Chichester's bishop, who was the most saintly character of his time. Unlike so many early Churchmen, he was not a statesman; he was just a good and pure man who, though he was a bishop in a materialistic world, lived like one of the apostles. Perhaps he is the only Englishman who might be compared with St Francis of Assisi. He was a cause of some anxiety to his steward, for he was always giving away his money. On one occasion he went to see a prisoner in jail, and on his departure took good care to leave the door open!

I STOOD ON THE BAR GATE at Southampton and looked down over the town of Sir Bevis. It was a clear morning. There was a bustle along the narrow streets and in the air was the nearness of great ships.

An Atlantic liner lay at the dockside. Over the gangways swarmed porters carrying luggage. Men shouted and cleared a space as the huge cranes swung round lifting piles of boxes. There was the throb of imminent departure. Men looked at watches. Each second had its value. Smoke came from the funnels of the monster whose bulk was lifted above me, deck piled on deck. The sides of this ship were like the side of a cliff. From the high portholes gazed here and there a face like the face of a caveman looking down into a valley.

Someone shouted my name from the top of the mountain. Looking up, I saw a rich man known to me.

'Get a pass and come aboard!' he shouted.

In a few minutes I was sitting in a dove-grey boudoir like the reception-room of an exceptionally famous actress (only tidier), which this man called his cabin.

We went on a tour of inspection down endless paint-smelling corridors. He told me how many yards long they were, but I have forgotten. We went into a vast palm lounge, into a dining-room bigger than the dining-room of any hotel, into a swimming-pool, into a gymnasium full of electric horses, camels, rowing boats, cycles and machines designed to pommel the horrid stomachs of fat men.

Gold lifts shot up and down. Stewards ran here and there. Dazed-looking passengers wandered about wondering how they had taken the wrong turning and if they would ever find the way back to their cabins.

My friend, who is swiftly bored, left me: and I went down and down into the bowels of this grotesque hotel.

A siren blew.

'Visitors on shore, please!'

The great ship was ready to cross the Atlantic.

45

ABOVE Beaulieu
Palace House
RIGHT The New Forest

The siren laughed again with fiendish hoots; and slowly – so slowly – the ship moved with two tugs beneath her great bows.

A telegraph boy stood on the quay with his fist full of undelivered envelopes and his eyes, following the liner, full of injury and resentment. He was as ridiculous as a frog feeling annoyed about a volcano. But he whistled, jumped to his bicycle, and pedalled back with his bundle of farewells into the grey Town of Goodbye which men call Southampton.

HERE, IN BEAULIEU – they pronounce it Bewley – nothing happens or, it seems, could happen except the coming and going of the tide in the river, the budding and the falling of the leaves, the rising and the setting of the sun and the moon . . .

46

This is a strange, lonely place in the middle of the last of England's great forests. I am inclined to think that it is one of the strangest places I know. The people are slow Saxons, well-mannered, deferential people, with their wits about them and their tongues padlocked. Their ancestors most wisely took to cover when William Rufus came crashing through the bracken in search of the stag which – as you remember – led to a grave. They are still good at taking cover behind the barriers of their reticence. The place, like the people, encourages a delicious slowness. You feel that London with all its fret is not quite so important in the ultimate scheme of things as Mr Smith's new litter of pigs; and it seems to you, as you lean against a fence in portentous silence, that those things which men break their hearts upon are not worth so much in the long run as the sight of the moon tangled up in the boughs of a young birch wood. Heresy, of course!

It would be fatal to stay too long in Beaulieu; you would wish for nothing better than to lean over Mr Smith's pigsty or to stand by the mill stream and watch the stars grow bright in the evening.

I have been wondering, in the spell of this village, whether it is possible for the odour of Sanctuary to cling to a place.

This tiny hamlet with its magnificent abbey ruin was from 1204 to 1539 one of the chief places in England to which the murderer, the thief, the plotter, and the general fugitive from justice flew literally for his life. Once within the wall no one could touch him: 'the peace of the church' was over him like a shield, and the sheriff might bang on the great gates as loud as Judgement Day and the knights might ride round the wall as long as they liked with swords drawn, but the fox had gone to holy earth; he was as safe as though he had never sinned.

Through the Middle Ages, Beaulieu must have entertained one of the world's record assemblies of rogues and vagabonds; men who dared not take one step outside the walls. The white monks farmed the land and fished the river, singing High Mass every day in the lovely abbey church; and I suppose no one was startled or excited at so usual a sight as that of a man on a winded horse riding full tilt at the gate to join this queer brotherhood of the hunted. I imagine that the Abbot of Beaulieu owned a visitors' book rather like Scotland Yard's file of wanted faces.

All that remains of this old storm is a tall ruin in the light of that same moon on the banks of that same river. The evil seems to have gone from Beaulieu, but the feeling of Sanctuary remains: the feeling – it may seem a strange thing to say – that 'the peace of the church' is still over the fields, making something more than solitude.

The mouth of the Beaulieu River

The port of the little kingdom of Beaulieu is some three miles south along Beaulieu River; and it is called Buckler's Hard.

Figure-head at
Buckler's Hard

Buckler is the name of a man who lived there centuries ago, and Hard refers to the character of the river bank in this locality. Now, when you enter Buckler's Hard you feel at once the queer atmosphere which clings to a place in which men have expended great energy; the village seems to be resting after effort. The street, as wide as Regent Street, is only one hundred yards long. It ends, as if cut off suddenly, in green hummocks and mounds on which cattle graze.

Below this single street standing among fields, the ground falls gently to the banks of the Beaulieu River. The stream is wide at full tide, and at low exposes a great tract of shallow, reedy bank. Beyond the river, wood lies piled on wood to the sky-line.

When you walk beside the river you notice once again that evidence of a dead village buried under grass. Here are more green hummocks and mounds. Great timbers go down into the water, rotting and covered with weed. In the field are gigantic dips and hollows full of lush grass and flowers.

In those dips and on those rotting slipways once rested the stout oak-built ships which helped to found the British Empire. This unknown, forgotten village in Hampshire was once loud with the sound of forge hammers, here thousands of great oak trees were formed into ships of the line; and into the water of Beaulieu River was launched in 1781 the *Agamemnon*, a 64-gun ship of 1,384 tons burden, in which Nelson lost his right eye at the siege of Calvi.

One hundred and fifty years ago, John, Duke of Montagu, then lord of the manor, owned the sugar-producing island of St Vincent in the West Indies. His manor was stocked with fine oak trees, and his little port of Buckler's Hard was a free harbour – a legacy inherited from the old abbots of Beaulieu. A keen businessman, he thought it would be a fine thing if he could steal a little of the ship-building trade from Southampton and transplant it to Buckler's Hard. Between 1745 and 1808 about forty-four men-of-war were launched at Buckler's Hard.

I F SOULS IN HEAVEN gain any pleasure from looking through the golden bars to earth, men like old Thomas Sutton, who planted the Charterhouse in Smithfield, and men like that much more distant philanthropist, Bishop Henry de Blois, the grandson of William the Conqueror, who planted this hospice of St Cross in Hampshire, must feel an overwhelming happiness. The seed has grown and borne fruit century after century. Time, which wrecks the greatest monuments, has left such works unchanged – good deeds still shedding kindness in the world.

In the year 1136 Henry de Blois founded the Hospital of St Cross to shelter 'thirteen poor men, feeble and so reduced in strength that

they can hardly or with difficulty support themselves without another's aid'. They were to be provided 'with garments and beds suitable to their infirmities, good wheaten bread daily of the weight of 5 marks, and three dishes at dinner and one at supper suitable to the day, and drink of good stuff'. The hospital was also to give food and drink to poor wanderers who came to its gates.

St Cross is the oldest almshouse in England.

Such places are so steeped in the peace of unhurried years that they seem out of the world: you feel that the worries of life have ceased at the gates. On the west side of the lawns stand the houses of the Brethren, distinguished by tall chimneys, each house containing,

51

St Cross Hospital

like those of the Carthusians, two rooms, a pantry, and a garden.
Over the smooth grass, in the shadow of the gracious grey stones,
walk the ancient Brethren of St Cross.

'There's a waiting list as long as your arm,' said a smiling old
Brother. 'We are very lucky to end our days here. Would you care
to see the church?'

We went into one of the finest Transition-Norman churches I have
ever seen: a calm, majestic, splendidly proportioned church, with
great stone columns down the nave, vast as giant oak trunks.

The Brethren's Hall, where, for centuries, old men have eaten their
'mortrell' of 'was-tell' and milk, or herring pie and, sometimes, 'plum

broth', not forgetting of course their 'galiones' of small beer, is a building which dignifies the word charity. A study of charity through the ages is a good subject for a man with a taste to write it; and in this hall we are in touch with an age which gave nobly and gladly. Side by side with hideous cruelty and callousness existed this pious love for 'the poor of Christ'. There is a raised hearth in the centre of the hall round which the Brethren gathered at a charcoal fire. At one end of the room is a delicious gallery in which the minstrels played on great occasions.

THE RAIN CEASED IN THE NIGHT and, awakening early as one does in a strange room, I saw a brightness behind the blind that told me the sun was shining. Winchester was not yet awake. It was that lovely time in early spring when the world, it seems, is swept and garnished for a festival. As I walked through the empty streets, I wondered when the citizens of Winchester, now snuggling down into that last self-indulgent half-hour of bed, would realise their folly and, opening their doors, come tumbling out to go a-Maying. A thrush was singing in the cathedral limes and the sun, still low in the east, played early morning tricks in the streets, gilding unexpected places, casting improbable shadows. It was mellow over that old school which has sent so many men clearly labelled into the world. You can generally tell them at a glance, especially in the law courts, when they rise for the prosecution and, with a kind of cold pleasure, stab the rhetoric of the defence with an intellectual instrument forged at Winchester – 'aut disce, aut discede, manet sors tertia caedi'; some-one who knew Winchester (it may have been Wren) carved that on the wall of 'School' in 1683.

I went on, thinking that if one were looking for the germ of the British Empire, it is to be found in this quiet little city of Winchester. The princes of this city emerged as the Kings of Wessex, after their long war with the Danes, and later became the Kings of England; and it was the royal city of Winchester which was truly the very heart of England until Westminster Hall and the Abbey gathered round them the royal city of a new England.

I went to see the Great Hall of the Castle of Winchester, all now left of the royal palace that stood on the traditional Castle of King Arthur. How the prestige of Winchester endured! When King Henry VII wished to strengthen his hereditary claim to the throne in 1486, he could think of nothing better to his purpose than to bring his queen to Winchester in order that the heir to the throne might be born in the Castle of King Arthur.

I expected to see Norman work, but it is early English, aisles, dormer windows and high, slim pillars of Purbeck marble.

53

The Round Table of King Arthur has hung for over five hundred years on the walls of Winchester Hall. It is first mentioned by John Hardyng in 1378:

ABOVE King Arthur's table
LEFT Winchester Cathedral

> The rounde Table of Wynchester beganne
> And there it ended and there it hangeth yet.

Henry VIII brought the Emperor Charles V, when he was visiting England in 1522, to see this table, which he exhibited as one of the most interesting sights in the kingdom. It cannot, of course, be the Round Table of legend, but it is a most fascinating piece of carpentry. It was repainted in Tudor times, and it shows King Arthur sitting crowned in Tudor robes. A point in favour of the legend is that it is quite large enough to seat the king and his twenty-four knights.

3 Oxford and northwards

OXFORD IS ONE OF THOSE PLACES which encourages the art of valediction. How natural it is that a young man, or a young woman, having spent some years in its shelter, should address a few polite words of farewell before turning towards the bleaker regions of reality.

Strangely enough, this custom of saying goodbye to Oxford seems to have been inaugurated by Queen Elizabeth. When Her Majesty was leaving Oxford in 1592, she stopped her coach before it went down the hill to Wheatley, and turning to the dreaming spires she addressed them:

'Farewell, farewell, dear Oxford,' she said, 'God bless thee and increase thy sons in number, holiness and virtue.'

It would be impertinent for a stranger to presume to judge the holiness or virtue of Oxford, but he is at liberty to say that Her Majesty's other command has been obeyed: Oxford's sons have increased in such numbers, and each one possesses either a motor car or a bicycle, that it is now difficult to cross the road except at a hunted run. No other town of its size in England leaves upon the mind such an impression of congestion. It may be possible to find in the remote depths of some college, possibly in its cellars, a place where one might be tolerably safe from assassination, or at least out of earshot of bicycle bells, motor cycles, and those sudden harsh rending noises, as if an eighty-foot giant has torn his trousers, which indicate that a lorry is changing gear.

I went to the Trout Inn, which stands in the shadow of Godstow Bridge. The sound of water rushing down between the gates of the weir ceases neither by day nor night. Among the beauties of this old building is a moss-grown roof of Stonesfield slate, perhaps the most attractive roofing material ever used in England. I would rather see it than the finest thatch or the most mellowed tiles. One of the

Oxford's dreaming spires

57

Burford: '*All the old villages in this limestone belt are made of fine stone, some of them dark, some honey-brown.*'

pleasures of travelling in England is the crossing of geological boundaries into new scenery and to fresh styles in ancient architecture.

All the old villages in the limestone belt of Oxfordshire are made of fine stone, some of them dark, some honey-brown, and those buildings which, like the inn at Godstow, are also roofed with stone, seem to me the most perfect of all. Mellowed by centuries of wind and rain, they collect the seeds of many mosses and even ferns, which thrive until they form a soft greenish-yellow carpet through which the silver-grey of the stones can still be seen.

The inn at Godstow is familiar to generations of Oxford men, and it is good to know that popularity has not spoilt it. There is a touch of 'Alice in Wonderland' about it. The rooms are low, dark and heavily beamed. The bar, full of old oak and settles, is crowded like a museum with rustic objects and sporting relics.

Generations of undergraduates have filled the place with laughter and talk, with exuberance and a youthful extravagance of mind, so that I did not know whether the old house itself or the people who run it were responsible for the impression that it is a quaint repository of much that is precious and lovable in the English character, among which I would mention humour, toleration, and a casual acceptance of eccentricity.

The place overflowed with hearty young men, pint pots in hand. Across the meadows came others who had walked from Oxford, and still more came by car and bicycle, until the terrace by the water was crowded with a new and, in my opinion, satisfactory generation.

EIGHT MILES OR SO to the north of Oxford, reposing in June sunshine, was Woodstock. Here is a town that in some almost miraculous way has escaped the vulgarities of our age and lives in calm and dignity, a standing memorial to the virtue of patronage, for it has grown up in the shadow of kings and dukes. Some houses gaze at each other across wide streets: some are Tudor, some Queen Anne, others are Georgian or Victorian; and all these styles harmonise and show their relationship one to the other, so that they remind you of a family of several generations gathered in the same room.

Woodstock is, of course, a name famous in history, for in the neighbouring park once stood the Manor of Woodstock, one of the most ancient royal residences in the country. It was the traditional scene of 'Rosamond's Bower' and almost all the sovereigns of England visited the place until the time of Queen Anne, when the old palace was pulled down.

Before Elizabeth was queen she was imprisoned at Woodstock, suspected of plotting against her sister, Queen Mary, and she visited

The Thames at
Godstow

the town on happier occasions after she had ascended the throne. On one such occasion she was presented with the best pair of gloves that Woodstock could make.

The most noted industry of the town in the old days was delicate steel work made from the nails of old horseshoes. These were melted down, and the metal apparently treated in some way before it was wrought into a variety of objects. A chain of Woodstock steel weighing only two ounces was once sold in France for £170. It was the rise of the cheap metal industries of Birmingham and Sheffield that killed the Woodstock steel work, of which not a trace now remains.

The great sight of Woodstock is the Palace of Blenheim, which belongs to the Duke of Marlborough. The park is always open to the public, and the entrance to it is in the town. I passed beneath a vast triumphal archway into a deer park of nearly three thousand acres, where miles of grassland are varied by giant oaks and cedars. After walking for some time down a long avenue, I saw Blenheim Palace ahead, and, although I knew roughly what to expect, the sight shook me. That enormous mass of Renaissance stone planted with a terrific air of emphasis and conviction in an English park, and looking from a

Woodstock, Thomas
Chaucer's house

distance like a town that has lost its way, is one of England's most splendid fantasies. The scale on which Blenheim is built exceeds anything I have ever seen. Even photographs give no true idea of it. And as I drew nearer, I gazed in still greater astonishment, thinking that no better proof exists in all the world of the things an architect can do, given a great patron, a moment of national emotion, and a free hand.

I remembered a sentence, one that implies a profound and pessimistic knowledge of architects and their ways, in Churchill's great book, *Marlborough, His Life and Times*. 'According to a deep law of nature,' wrote Mr Churchill, 'the architect's estimate of £100,000 fell far short of the realised expense.'

Few people will dispute that Marlborough was the greatest military leader in English history. He took the field at the head of the allied armies to oppose the determination of Louis XIV to dominate the world. He humbled the power of France in four great battles: the first was at Blenheim, in Bavaria, in 1704. When the news of this victory reached England, the country, wild with joy, decided to reward her captain-general with some great memorial. It was the wish of Queen Anne that the offering should take the form of the old royal Manor of Woodstock, in whose park it was further decided by Queen and Parliament to build, at their joint cost, a grand house to be called the Palace of Blenheim.

The architect chosen to design this house was John Vanbrugh, a man intoxicated by stone. He was not only a great architect, but also a great dramatist. Some people would rather see one of his plays than one of his palaces.

Sarah, Duchess of Marlborough, was one of the most decisive and managing women of her time, and upon her fell the responsibility of watching this gigantic palace rise from the ground, for her husband was usually abroad winning battles. Sarah did not really like the idea of Blenheim. She would rather have had something to live in. But she knew that her husband's heart was set on the scheme; she knew that

Blenheim Palace

he thought of it, not as a house, but as an enduring monument that would last, if Vanbrugh built it, for a very long time. So she loyally superintended the building, opposing the architect whenever possible, and watching with alarm the operation of that 'deep law of nature', which steadily drove the cost of Blenheim from £100,000 to £300,000.

The palace took seventeen years to build, and the man for whom it was built never saw it completed. The seventeen years were years of quarrels between Sarah and the architect and the architect and the workmen, whose pay was often in arrears or not forthcoming at all.

Seventeen years is a long time for national gratitude to endure if there are bills to be met all the time, and it is not surprising, therefore, that Parliament refused to pay up. The Duke, still winning battles abroad, heard with dismay that his national memorial was likely to be burned down by angry workmen, and Vanbrugh sent him a note of the financial position: £220,000 had been paid by the Treasury; £42,000 was due to the workmen, and another £25,000 was needed to carry on; but no one was willing to advance a penny.

It is difficult to say what would have happened to Blenheim if Queen Anne had not succumbed to a fit of apoplexy in 1714; and no sooner was she dead than George I was in England, Marlborough was back in triumph, and the first man to be knighted by the new monarch was the architect, John Vanbrugh.

Work started again, this time at the Duke's cost and Vanbrugh once again flung himself with irrepressible vigour into the erection of his life's most monumental effort. For eight years the work continued. Immense new sums were spent; still the Palace was not completed. Then the Duke of Marlborough died! The man for whom all this magnificence was made never lived there, never enjoyed it, never got anything out of it except a grandiose dream of posthumous fame.

The end of the story is that the Duchess Sarah, having been left a fortune by her husband (as Vanbrugh said 'to ruin Blenheim her own way') got rid of him and employed another architect.

Although she never liked the idea of Blenheim, so great was her devotion to Marlborough that she carried out the scheme to its bitter end, as he would have wished her to do.

I TOOK TO THE ROAD AGAIN one hot day in June, and the road led between high Warwickshire hedges to that place of blessed memory, the Forest of Arden. The spring which I had seen advance, leaf by leaf, flower by flower, was now merged in the rich splendour of summer. The trees cast a deep shade; the corn was high in the fields.

And as I smoked my pipe in that good old inn on the high road at Henley-in-Arden I was seized, suddenly and surprisingly, with the desire for one of those sentimental journeys which occasionally afflict the souls of men in the middle thirties.

It is an amusing error to revisit a place which thrilled us when we were very young. I seem to remember Stratford-on-Avon as a quiet little heaven where it was always May, with the nightingales shaking silver in the dark trees at night and the Avon mooning under Hugh of Clopton's grand old bridge. And I was terribly young. I used to rise with the sun and walk over dripping meadows with their wrong-way-round shadows, the king-cups shaking dew over my boots, and I

would read Shakespeare aloud to the astonishment of the cows, pausing transfixed in wonder (on an empty stomach) by such lines as – well, never mind. Only Youth knows; only Youth can achieve that passionate intensity.

I drove between those well-loved Warwick hedges, through a perfect death-rattle of motor traffic, into Stratford. My quiet old Stratford was suffering from a rush of trippers. Coaches from everywhere were piled up in the square; half the cars of the Midlands were either coming or going; and the hotel was full of long-legged girls from America, and sallow fathers and spectacled mothers.

They gave me a bedroom called 'Love's Labour Lost' – all the rooms in this hotel are Shakespeareanised – and, as it overlooked the street, I sat a while watching more Americans arrive and thinking how amused Shakespeare would have been. Stratford's fame rests on Shakespeare; much of its prosperity rests on the fact that it is a social disgrace in America not to have rushed through Stratford. This town is the very core of the heart of the American's England.

I found one thing unchanged in Stratford: a mossy seat on the high wall of Holy Trinity churchyard overlooking the Avon. This is, to my mind, one of the supremely English views. It seems as you sit there with the willows dipping to the river, beyond, on the opposite bank,

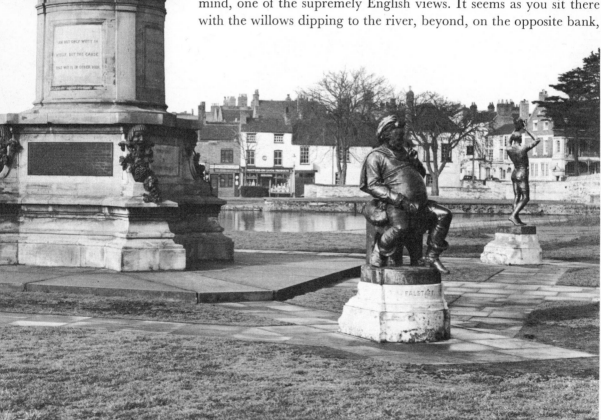

Stratford: the Shakespeare monument;

Holy Trinity Church

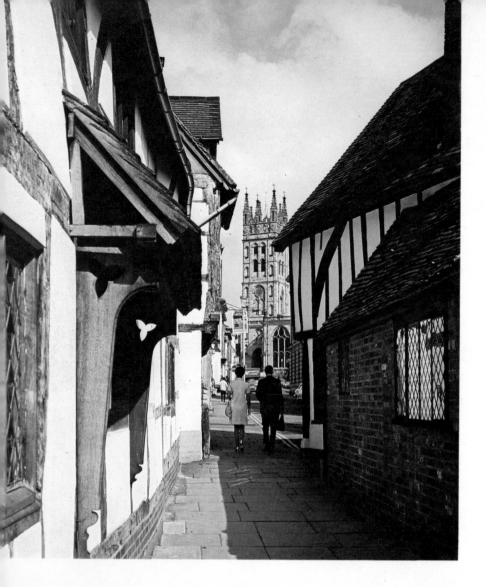

great freckled meadows, and in the air the sound of the water rushing past the old mill, that all the beauty and peace of the Warwickshire country-side have been packed into one riverscape. Between the tombstones grow vast yew trees. It is so right that Shakespeare's bones should lie in this quiet church . . . now and again from the thin spire a bell tells the time lazily; the tall avenue of lime trees moves in the wind.

Warwick Castle. You see it from the bridge, lying high on its cliff bowered among trees, shining in the Avon, the two machicolated towers to the right. Generally the bridge is crowded with trippers. Someone always says: 'That's one of the finest views in England'; which is true.

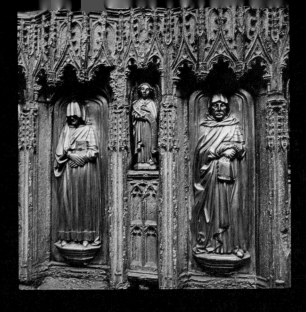 

I stood there alone. I suppose that Warwick Castle is, after Windsor, the most famous and the most beautiful in England.

A guide met me at the Barbican, and we walked past vivid green lawns such as you will see in no other country in the world, till we came to the grey bulk of the castle, with a blankness about the windows which seemed to say that the earl was not at home.

The Great Hall of Warwick Castle is, although extensively and carefully restored, one of the glories of England. In old days the Earls of Warwick used to ride in on horseback, scattering the rushes, and, dismounting, draw a dagger and help themselves to the ox or the sheep which was roasting before the great log fire.

How many Americans, I wonder, stand in this hall every year with their faith in England justified? It is California's ideal of an English nobleman's home. Its influence can, I think, be traced on the films.

We admired the armour, also the giant cooking pot called Guy's Punch Bowl, an enormous cauldron that holds a hundred and twenty gallons, made in the fourteenth century for Sir John Talbot of Swannington. There is a legend that when an Earl of Warwick comes of age Guy's Punch Bowl is filled and emptied three times.

Is there a fairer scene in Warwickshire than the view of the Avon from the drawing-rooms? The river runs far below between green banks, cascading over a weir.

69

These rooms are delicious. They are packed with treasures. Holbein, Rubens, Van Dyck, Lely are frame to frame on the walls. The lighting is mellow. Little gilt shields illuminate the canvases and reflect their richness.

It was growing dark when I entered the Beauchamp Chapel, which takes the breath away with its beauty. I can compare it only with Henry VII's Chapel in Westminster Abbey and King's College, Cambridge. The great Richard Beauchamp lay with his bare head in a tilting helm and his hands raised above his breast. I remember the story of the disaster that overtook the Earl's body in the seventeenth century. The floor of the chapel fell in, and the body was found inside the tomb marvellously preserved. The women of Warwick, it is said, seized the hair and worked it into rings . . .

The light faded moment by moment. I went out into the streets of Warwick, those quiet, attractive streets that have not lost a look of other days, conscious that a man might spend a month here and not exhaust the memories that lie so thickly beside the green banks of the Avon.

IT IS DIFFICULT TO KNOW in Kenilworth where Elizabeth ends and Walter Scott begins. I went there on one of those hot sleepy mid-summer afternoons, when the heat throws a haze low over the meadows and stones are hot to the hand.

This rambling, chocolate-red ruin fills me with a greater sense of desolation than any other ruin I have seen in England. Tudor England, in which it reached its prime, is, as time goes, only yesterday. The faces, the philosophy, the poetry, the deeds, even the love letters, of the people who moved through that age are still as fresh in our memories as the faces and the thoughts of friends. While many a Saxon and a Norman building stands perfect in England with the mistakes of the builders' axes still clean in the stone, this Kenilworth flings its tattered walls to the skies, and its once grand stairways end in thin air, and the green grass lies in great hummocks over the tilt yard.

This ruin is one of the tragedies. Had it only survived, as other Tudor buildings contemporary with it have survived, Kenilworth Castle would be without a peer of its kind in the historic monuments of England.

I SUPPOSE NO ONE DARES to write about Coventry without mentioning motor cars, so having done this in the first sentence, we will leave it there. The interesting fact about Coventry is, to my mind, not cycles or cylinders, but women. Coventry has always been lucky with women, and should, therefore, be England's happiest city.

Kenilworth Castle

Womenfolk of Coventry

It begins with an old legend that when Coventry was in its infancy the eleven thousand virgins of Cologne arrived there on a kind of spiritual Cook's tour. They stayed awhile, illuminating the village with their piety, and, departing, left eleven thousand virtues to be shared by successive generations of their own sex in Coventry. If any city in the kingdom has a more beautiful story or has paid a sweeter compliment to its womenfolk, I have yet to hear about it.

It is interesting, to descend from fiction to strange fact, that Coventry has a remarkable feminine roll of honour: St Osburg, Lady Godiva, Isabella, Margaret of Anjou, the sisters Botoner, who built the spire, Joan Ward, the Lollard Martyr, Mrs Siddons, George Eliot, Ellen Terry.

I was not a bit surprised, on entering the city, that the eleven thousand virgins seem still in possession. One, shopping with a Sealyham at the corner of Hertford Street, had inherited far more than her fair share, if beauty is a virtue.

72

Lady Godiva has always attracted me. She is, of course, the leading lady in Coventry's history. I do not care much for the modern version of her ride, which, in an excess of Victorian modesty, makes her agonised by the shame of her ordeal. I prefer the first written account done by Roger of Wendover, somewhere about AD 1230, which, to any man who knows and admires the grim recklessness of a woman who has made up her mind, rings down seven centuries with the tone of truth. According to him Godiva wasted no time in remorse, or wondering what the Robinsons would say. She just 'loosened her hair, thus veiling her body, and then, mounting her horse and attended by two knights, she rode through the market seen of none, her white legs nevertheless appearing; and, having completed her journey, returned to her husband rejoicing . . . '

BIRMINGHAM . . .

The train spins on over the points. Men in the dining-car fidget with luggage, as the promise of Edgbaston, home and beauty illuminates their honest features. A talkative commercial traveller considers that with luck he will have time to absorb his fifth whisky and soda. And the train spins on.

The commercial traveller puts down an empty glass on the green table and says:

'Birmingham is unlike any other town. They make every blessed thing but ships . . . from pins to railway carriages. That is why Birmingham can never feel unemployment like a city with one big staple industry: there is always so much happening.'

He rises and takes down a suitcase.

'It's a tough spot, too,' he says. 'If you can sell things in Brum you can sell them anywhere on earth.'

He takes down another suitcase.

'Hard-headed lot!' he says.

He pulls down a third, and, casting a cautious glance round the dining-car, whispers confidentially:

'Rotten hole – I hate it! Goes to bed at ten!'

The train dives through a tunnel and out into New Street Station, prompt to the minute – two hours from Euston!

I step out on the platform with the feeling that some kind of a thrill is due: the faint thrill, perhaps, of meeting a self-made man who by hard work, self-denial, acuteness and the ordinary human virtues has pulled himself into fame. Birmingham.

Down the steep hill of the Bull Ring, where a market began in Saxon times, is a church. It is, perhaps, generous to believe that more than two per cent of one million people have been inside more than twice. In the chancel four stone men sleep, three in full armour, one

73

Birmingham,
St Martin's and
the Bull Ring

74

in full canonicals, the de Berminghams, the old lords of the manor. They lie, inexpressibly remote in the silence, deserted, forgotten, the men who pegged out the claim, who had no idea that they had founded anything larger than a green village.

It takes you ten minutes to realise that as a city Birmingham does not exist. It is a myth. No city with a million population has greater municipal enterprises and fewer evidences of civic grandeur. But it takes days to realise that if Birmingham is not a city in the sense that squares are wide and streets majestic, it is a series of industrial encampments, the greatest workshop the world has ever known.

Soon after dawn there is a whine in the air. The early buses are running. Each day they irrigate with human life forty-three thousand acres of dull streets. They drive on with their packed loads, pausing at little street corners, where platoon after platoon from the great battalion of workers descends and makes off to the day's task.

I look at their hands: capable, grimy hands born to control machinery, made to fashion objects, to beat new life into white-hot metal: to do a million tasks for which the world has need.

There are girls: small, sturdy girls with nimble fingers practised in quick work in a packing room, in dabbing a speck of paint on a thousand objects which, one by one, go past them on a moving band all day long. Sprightly, smart girls, loud of voice, independent, laughing, giggling, full of life that must be repressed throughout the long day's task.

As you go on and on through a drab uniformity – district after district each with its own shops – it is possible to trace how wave after wave of manufacturing prosperity added acreage to Birmingham; a city with a Georgian core and a Victorian red-brick casing.

So you travel to the outer crust of ugliness, where on the very outskirts of Birmingham stand those great camps of industry, little towns in themselves, where small houses cluster round a huge mass of stone and brick from which tall chimney stacks spire to the sky. Here men live side by side with the machine. Beyond lie the green fields and the hills, wondering how long it will be before the great footsteps of Birmingham stride up and go on down the valley.

It is one of the virtues of Birmingham that the grandfathers of so many prosperous natives arrived in the city a century and a half ago with nothing on them but a shirt. The only aristocracy is the aristocracy of successful commerce. Grandfather went to work, and soon some one was working for him. His sons became rich and carried on; and now their sons, having been to Oxford, possess all those advantages necessary for the wrecking of the apple cart – or a greater success, a wider field . . .

People at work

Now, perhaps, you understand why Birmingham is a city of three or four short, select streets. Not only has it been too busy to look grand and important: it is also lacking in local millionaires anxious to speculate in putting up big property. It is a city of moderate wealth, of moderate men. Money is perhaps more evenly spread here than in any other big industrial city.

Birmingham is not a show place – it is a work place, a useful city, a city that cares little for appearance but much for results, a city that looks at life in terms of material achievement. A great sense of beauty or wide learning will always be unhappy in Birmingham; for Birmingham is a great machine that knows only production.

4 The Peak District to Lancashire

IN THE QUIET DERBYSHIRE VILLAGE of Eyam, men still talk about the Plague of London as though it had happened last week. Eyam is the last place in England with a vivid memory of the terrible pestilence of 1665.

Eyam is a mile-long street of fortress-like stone houses set in a cosy cleft of the wild Peakland moors. There is a church, a manor-house behind a wall, and the remains of the village stocks. I went into the church, where the elderly caretaker began to talk, as they all do in Eyam, of the plague:

'We used to leave our money in the well, where the water washed it clean,' she said. 'And people from other villages would bring food for us and take the money out of the well. We used to put vinegar in the water to disinfect it. It was terrible. Every one was frightened of catching the Plague . . .'

(She might have been talking about that year's influenza!)

The great Plague of London, which came before the Fire of London, lives for us now only in the diary of Pepys, in the fine journalism of Defoe's *Plague Year*. So many things have happened to London since the reign of Charles II that the Plague is not even a memory! But it was the last thing that happened to Eyam!

This is the story.

In the autumn of 1665, a box of clothes was sent from London to a tailor in this village. They were damp. The servant who dried them at a fire became ill and died of the plague. So also did others in the house. The horrible thing had taken root among the clean, windy moors of Derbyshire.

No one knew where the next plague death would occur. No one knew when he or she might develop the swelling symptoms which were literally a death warrant. People wanted to get away, to reach the windy moors, to put miles behind them and the village which had suddenly become a place of horror.

'In Eyam men still talk . . .'

79

Then an extraordinary thing happened which must give Eyam a foremost place among the courageous villages of England.

The rector, William Mompesson, saw that the stampede from Eyam might spread the plague through the north of England. He assembled the villagers and persuaded them to remain and defy the pestilence. He promised that he would stand by them to the end. He drew a line round the village a mile from its centre, and beyond this boundary no man, woman, or child from Eyam was to move. At various points along the line were established food dumps. People from other villages would come up at given times with supplies, which they left on the boundary. So Eyam was fed.

When Mompesson appealed to the courage of his parishioners three hundred and fifty people remained in Eyam with him. The plague continued for over twelve months, and when it ended, as it did suddenly, two hundred and sixty-seven had died. Only eighty-three remained to tell the story of a year's horror.

Eyam,
Plague Cottages

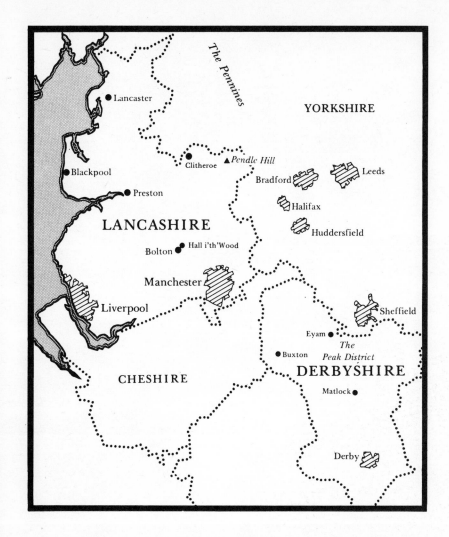

Surely there are few villages in England which can point to a braver story . . .

It is difficult to visualise that year of death. The old cottages are so small and snug. Children laugh and play about the street. Untroubled faces look through the very windows which saw, three centuries ago, the passing of the plague carts; a wife going to bury her husband or a husband his wife.

I think the most touching plague relic in Eyam is a little cluster of graves in a field some distance from the village. They are protected from wandering cattle by a low small stone wall. They are very lonely, with the wind blowing over them, the green moss eating into them, and about them still an air of haste and disaster. Among them are the graves of the Hancock family, seven of whom died in eight days.

Stone walls in Derbyshire

82

IF A LONDONER CAN IMAGINE Dartmoor moved into Essex he will have some idea of the meaning of the Peak District to the crowded industrial cities of the north. At the very doors of Manchester, and on the east Sheffield, are miles of the wildest country in England. Men and women from these cities can be lost in untamed hills in less time than it takes a Londoner to ride from the Bank to Hammersmith.

The ease with which the workers of Manchester and Sheffield can reach open country would be astonishing to any southerner who does not know this part of England. A Cockney in search of a similar escape into the same refreshing wilderness would have to go to Devonshire! Every weekend thousands of men and women leave the northern cities to fill their lungs with the sharp moorland air, for Peakland invigorates the body and the mind of the industrial north.

As I took the Cat and Fiddle Road over the hills – one of the highest roads in England – I met in a sudden and unexpected manner this wild thing that is at the very heart of the north country.

It was raining, a fine persistent drizzle. The road twisted gracefully round and up to a desolate land of peaty moors, cut across by low limestone walls, brown and shining in the wet. Curlews were flying over the brownish grass, sheep grazed mournfully above the walls, and the clouds, flying low, steamed gently across the crests of the hills, so that I was continually running in and out of mists.

Matlock Bath

So I climbed slowly on, the road hugging the edge of the hill. The map told me that I was twelve hundred feet above sea-level. I stopped my car and looked back across the distant panorama of long hills folded one upon another against the weeping sky; a grim, forbidding landscape. There was not one sign of human life.

Suddenly the rain became chilled. Far off to the left a moor sloped away dusted with white. It looked as though it had been sprinkled with lime. Still there was no sign of the storm. I looked to the right and there I saw it! Snow was blowing before the wind in wild eddies and spirals. It was blowing down to the distant moors which showed

dark and green through the moving whiteness. At a point far below, the white flakes vanished and fell as rain.

I climbed on. Snow began to fall, timidly at first, very slowly. The flakes became more frequent as I advanced. It was bitterly cold. Very still.

The highest (but one) inn in England stood in the very teeth of the gale on the highway. The snow cut across its chimneys, drifted against door and window frames. I had left an April world and had come, in a few short miles, to the depth of winter.

How the wind sprang up as I splashed along the exposed road towards Buxton! It tore at the windscreen, it held back my car, which shook itself and rocked in the sideways gusts that threatened to lift us and fling us to the rocks beneath.

The road dropped. So did the wind. The snow was melting. The grass was green. I had left Derbyshire's little Switzerland behind me. I passed a house with a garden full of flowers.

In Buxton the streets had dried after a shower. The snow-storm seemed like a dream. I looked back at the hills. It was true after all. Right at the top was a little patch of white the size of a saucer!

I CAME INTO MANCHESTER over a road as hard as the heart of a rich relation.

It was that time between dusk and the full blaze of electric light when the streets of Manchester fill with a curious uniform blueness which I have seen in no other city in the world. The streets are high jet-black banks. Between them flows this blue river, the colour of those large expensive Colmar grapes which one buys for people in hospital. It seems as though the smoke has in some way become damp and is hanging in the air.

I have been told that it always rains in Manchester. This is a lie; it had just stopped.

Manchester was going home after the day's work, not violently as London does, but leisurely, with calm. I came to a central blaze of light where Queen Victoria, sunk – I might even say collapsed – in a hopeless depression, sat regarding Manchester with the utmost disapproval. This place, I was told, is called Piccadilly.

And against the lit windows of Piccadilly was an exciting move-ment of crowds, the flash and twinkle of bright stockings. Certain streets in Manchester die at six every night, while others remain alive until eleven. The dead ones are dark; the live ones are brilliant with the gold windows of the closed shops. Manchester is as London would look if you can imagine lower Oxford Street and the Strand marching up into the City and settling down haphazardly in the neighbourhood of Lombard Street and Tower Hill. Manchester is an

PREVIOUS PAGES
Monsal Dale;
Burbage Brook,
Derbyshire

86

ABOVE Manchester

87

elusive city; one is always searching for its centre and never finding it.

Next day it was raining. The rain came down with enthusiasm.

In the hotel lounge I met a Spaniard who had come all the way from a sunny land to see a man in Manchester about some oranges.

A faint air of exile filled the lounge. We were all strangers who had come to Manchester to see somebody about something. Two men at the next table were talking German. On the left an honest Manchester man was having a terrible time with a client from the Levant.

'I know Manchester,' said a Spaniard. 'This rain!' He made a wide circle with his cigar which included the whole of Lancashire, and shrugged his shoulders. 'If you in England had a hot climate you would not be the great commercial nation you are. You concentrate against your climate. It gives you energy. It strengthens you. Look how big and hearty are the men of Manchester and how full of jokes. They have to be! Now in the south where I come from . . .'

There can be no city on earth in which so many funny (and almost funny) stories are told every day of the year. A Manchester man thinks nothing of keeping you out in the rain for half an hour while he tells you the story which you told him yesterday. Whenever you see two or three sitting together you can be certain that one of them

Spinning a yarn

is spinning the yarn. The loud laughter of Manchester men is in fine contrast to the weeping skies under which they live.

In Deansgate is a Gothic building set at a slight angle to the road, so that it seems to be as if about to retire to a monastery. It looks, among the shops and offices by which it is surrounded, like a shy saint in a crowd. It is the John Rylands Library. This is Manchester's greatest contrast. This is a little peaceful acre in the miles of buying and selling given over to the other things.

The most remarkable fact about it is that Manchester owed this library to a woman. It is the only great library in the world founded by a woman: it is the only great library which owes its existence to the love of a woman for the memory of her husband.

John Rylands made money in Manchester. He died, leaving Mrs Rylands with the responsibility of great wealth and the desire to erect a monument to his memory. How this woman planned her scheme, sought the best advice, the best architect, bought the famous Spencer collection for a quarter of a million – as a beginning – how she watched every detail of the enterprise, is vastly more interesting to me than the history of the Rylands fortune.

I imagine, after studying the shrewd Puritan face of John Rylands,

The Rylands Library

'Manchester will be
the last city in
England to go dry.'

that nothing in Manchester would probably surprise him more, could he come back, than the John Rylands Library!

In universities all over the world Manchester means not cotton but this library, and it is interesting to remember how often in history commercial capitals have produced great centres of learning, beginning with Alexandria, by way of Florence to Venice, three great trade centres of the ancient and the medieval world. It is surely a fine instance of historical repetition that since the discovery of the Americas moved the commercial centre of the world from the lagoons of Venice to the wet hills of Lancashire, a library constructed on the grand scale should have found its way to Manchester.

You go up a fine Gothic staircase into a rich brown cathedral of books. The Rylands Library is the colour of Chester Cathedral. Its great nave adapted to books, beyond each arch of it a little nest of shelves; its cloistered corridors, its stone fan vaulting, its windows, make you catch your breath, for here is that rare thing, a perfect modern Gothic building, exquisite in proportion, decoration, material, and perfectly adapted to its ends.

90

The public houses are crowded in Manchester on a Saturday night. Manchester will be the last city in England to go dry! (Norwich will, I think, stand by her to the end!) Pianos play! In all the main streets of Manchester there is the sound of song. A large woman goes to the piano and sings 'Annie Laurie' with great expression. There is applause. All the time the door is opening and shutting, and the barman's tray is awash in beer.

A GALE FROM AMERICA was delivering itself in the Mersey. Beautiful women were being blown up Lord Street in a most enchanting way, fighting and winning each corner.

I, who have lived in the solid self-assurance of Manchester for many days, felt as the gale hit me that I had escaped from a directors' to a lovers' meeting. Manchester – a man among the cities of the earth – inspires admiration, respect, loyalty even, but – how easy to fall in love with Liverpool, this elusive, moody city, so full of variety, beauty; so full of warm vitality.

The queer thought came to me as I walked the streets that the City of London was taking a holiday by the sea. There is about Liverpool something strangely London-like and poised: I find it in her men, her women, and her streets. There is an elegance here which I think exists in few places outside the capital. Liverpool has rubbed off her rough corners against the map of the world.

'Oh,' said the secretaries of three important businessmen, 'Mr So-and-so's in London today!'

Half the lifetime of Liverpool is spent in the Euston express!

The sound of the Great Dock Road is the voice of Liverpool. It is more than a road: it is the barometer of commerce.

All the produce of the world goes by upon the Great Dock Road. There is cotton for Lancashire, tobacco for Nottingham, metals for Birmingham, wool for the north country, raw material which will find its way into the far-spread intricate machinery of British manufacture. More than a third of British exports pass along the Great Dock Road.

The longer you study it the more fascinating it becomes. The peoples of the earth have laboured to fill its wagons. You identify the origin of boxes and crates as the lorries go past: a name here, a sign there: oranges from Jaffa, lemons from Naples, onions from Egypt, from Valencia, wool from the West, frozen meat from the Argentine ... just a few haphazard boxes in the convoy.

Over the high walls of the docks rise the warehouses, accepting and discharging their stores. Through the prison-like gates is many a glimpse of a ship home from sea, a long line of empty wagons

ABOVE Liverpool,
Oriel Chambers
RIGHT A teller on
the docks

FAR RIGHT
The Mersey and
the Liver Building

approaching for her cargo, or a ship loading, men swarming up her gangways, the cranes screaming, dipping their thin steel arms to the dockside and lifting boxes in an arc through the air to drop them into the omnivorous mystery of the hold.

At the back of the road is Liverpool, her fine buildings, her frequent touches of real grandeur, her many signs of elegant opulence, her busy men and women, split up and divided between a thousand endeavours, but most, in some way, vitally concerned with the long procession that winds all day along this road.

I stood beneath one of the Liver birds which crown the towers of the Liver building, and watched the sun set over Liverpool. Three miles off the mouth of the Mersey was cut across by a bright silver bar, which was the sea. I looked down over eight miles of docks: eight miles of great warehouses; eight miles of cranes; eight miles of ships at anchor.

Behind, mile after mile, the roofs, towers, chimneys of Liverpool lifted gently to the heights of Everton. The wind dropped, the mighty red sandstone cathedral, the greatest building of its kind since the Middle Ages, begun seventy years ago, rose up on its hill grandly like a great stronghold above the mist.

The sun went down in a stormy smother of cloud; little cargo boats, jet black against the bright silver of the Mersey, passed left and right; the last wagons going by below were just a faint vibration in the air, and from the Canada Dock a great ship with yellow funnels came slowly into midstream and took the way to America.

TWO MILES OUTSIDE BOLTON – a town of great character – the road twists up and round to Hall i'th'Wood. The wood has gone long ago, but the hall that once gleamed through the trees remains; a black and white Tudor country house, whose windows gaze out over Eagley Brook towards the tall mill chimneys of Bolton.

Every cotton spinner who has made money in Lancashire should put peas in his boots, wear a hair shirt, and go fasting to Hall i'th' Wood, for here in this lovely little house Samuel Crompton played his home-made violin and invented his famous spinning 'mule' – poor Samuel Crompton, the clever, irritable, unworldly man who died poor while his brains piled up fortunes for other men. The hall is now, thanks to the imagination and the money of the late Lord Leverhulme, the property of Bolton Corporation, and has been fitted up as an intelligent museum. It is not advertised. I suppose thousands pass through Bolton every day who have no idea that this place exists. And what an astonishment it is to the man who comes across it by chance! How surprising to find here in a little black-and-white

94

house overlooking the factories of Bolton two fine portraits by Peter Lely and two Van Dycks!

Hall i'th'Wood

When the Hall in the Wood ceased to be a country house towards the middle of the eighteenth century, it was let off as tenements to farmers and weavers. Among these tenants was the father of Samuel Crompton. From his earliest years Crompton was made to spin yarn on Hargreaves' spinning-jenny, and he hated it. It annoyed him. He thought it was the worst bit of machinery he had ever set eyes on. He was enraged by the ever-breaking ends of the thread, and one day he became so sick of Hargreaves that he decided to think out a better spinning machine.

He was forty-six years of age before his 'mule' was completed. It was called a mule because it was a cross between the water-frame and the spinning-jenny. It had both rollers and spindles, and its importance lay in the manufacture of a finer and stronger thread, which enabled the Lancashire weavers to rival the fine Indian muslins. This poor man in the tenement house thought out, alone and in the

95

still hours of the night (for he worked by night to obtain greater secrecy), an invention which was one of the chief means of transferring an ancient industry from the eastern to the western world.

Like all poor men who have done great things, Samuel Crompton starved himself for an idea. He made himself a fiddle and he played it in a Bolton theatre so that he might earn extra money to construct his machine.

The financial world smelt out a good thing in the 'Hall in the Wood Wheel', which was the first name given to the mule, and

Crompton was pried on. He hated that as much as he hated the breaking threads. He became more irritable than ever, and (how one would like to have given him legal advice!) he made one of the most absurd gestures in the history of invention and gave his mule to the public!

What a cynical mood fortune was in! Within thirty years from the invention of the mule five million spindles were being worked on Crompton's principle; and the inventor was still a poor man. Parliament was to be asked to vote him £20,000, but even here Crompton's bad luck became again evident. Spencer Perceval, the Prime Minister, was assassinated in the lobby of the House of Commons with the Crompton memorandum in his hand!

The inventor was eventually given £5,000, which he invested badly and was again penniless. He died, aged seventy-three, in receipt of a miserable £63 a year, and they buried him in the parish churchyard.

One more ironic thrust, and then Fate seemed to forget the family. In 1862 Bolton erected a statue to the man who helped to make it. The most notable figure on the platform was a poor old man of seventy-three, Crompton's surviving son.

I LOOKED AT THE SKY and knew that I wanted to climb a hill in wind or rain. I took the road to Pendle Hill beyond the town of Clitheroe, the best hill, I am informed, in all Lancashire. In fact, they say, and have said for centuries, 'Ingleborough, Pendle Hill, and Penyghent are the highest hills between Scotland and Trent', although I believe that the Ordnance Survey has proved this to be inaccurate...

Clitheroe is all that London imagines a Lancashire mill town is not. It has retained its ancient shape. The main street is still feudal-looking; it climbs up to a Norman castle and curves, as all good English lanes do, seeming to have been designed long ago in beautiful aimlessness by a herd of lost cattle. In Clitheroe you can see cotton mills and crocuses. To the south are Preston and Blackburn, to the west and to the north stretch the wild Lancashire fells, rolling hill against rolling hill as far as the eye can see.

Pendle Hill lifts his head beyond Clitheroe to a height of 1,813 feet. He is a real hill. He looks like 'a living creature stretched in sleep', a great whale of a hill jutting out sharply over the valley which he guards. This hill is to Lancashire almost as the Wrekin is to Shropshire; it is the one great physical feature of Lancashire steeped in local sentiment.

Now the wind comes over Pendle like a storm at sea. Pendle seems to have its own private supply of wind. When the rest of the landscape lies at peace the south wind tears over Pendle Hill in a splendid fury, and the colour of this hill is deep brown.

As you begin to climb in the steep track of a watercourse your feet strike chips of grey limestone, and Pendle smells good, on a sunny morning with the wind racing over it, of clean grass, heather, and wet vegetation.

Half-way up, unless you are in good training, you collapse grate-fully on a hummock and feel proud of yourself as you look back down the lonely hillside at the chequer-board of green pasture lands, so neat, so smoothly green, that merge gracefully into the blueness of the Yorkshire moors. Or you swear to give up cigarettes as the wind of Pendle takes you by the throat, as the height of Pendle hits you above the knee, as the wild beauty of Pendle adds another beat to your heart . . .

Near the summit the wind ceases suddenly. There are parts of Pendle over which it skips with a shrill whistle; you can hear it, but you cannot feel it until you climb up to the summit, where a post vibrates; and here the wind comes for you suddenly with an angry whistle anxious to hurl you back far down into the green valley from which you came.

FOUR MILES OF BOARDING-HOUSES – waiting. Hotels, big and small – waiting. Furnished apartments, whose windows are like wide, eager eyes – waiting. Three piers, from whose extremities small boys catch dabs – waiting. Miles of yellow sand – waiting. The Tower – waiting. The Wheel, with its wide circle of empty cars – waiting. Hundreds of shops full of broadly comic postcards, full of 'Presents from Blackpool', full of Blackpool rock, cafés, restaurants, dance-halls, cinemas, theatres – all waiting for the Lancashire 'wakes', and for the deluge of free men and women who will soon descend on Blackpool like a riot migrating to the sea coast.

Blackpool is just on the edge of its season. It is about to make sufficient money in three months to keep it for a year. The land-ladies of Blackpool have 'welcome' written not only on the mat but also on their faces; and men with paint pots wander about the town putting the final touches to England's greatest experiment in organised pleasure.

Blackpool is the logical result of Lancashire. It is the silver lining to all the clouds. It is as eloquent of Lancashire as the mills of Bolton and Oldham: it is Lancashire's idea of the earthly paradise.

There are millions of people all over the north of England who have been saving up for the past twelve months for a glorious week's fling at Blackpool.

Blackpool,
the Tower and
Central Pier

The 'wakes' are something we do not understand in the south. They are a contradiction of the northerner's traditional thrift. He is thrifty, but he can be open-handed. He arrives in Blackpool with his holiday money, and he spends every penny, and goes home broke to start all over again. But he carries back with him the memory of a week's careless affluence. He has known a week free from the nagging humiliation of slender means. He has scattered his pounds, and pence, nobly like a millionaire; but with much greater satisfaction!

5 The Lakes to Durham

ONE OF THE MOST UNLUCKY THINGS that can happen to a man travelling from Lancaster to Carlisle through the Lake country is a wet day. There is no happy medium about a wet day in the Lakes. The rain falls with a deliberate enthusiasm. If it stops it is through sheer weariness. Then it is succeeded by a white mist that wipes out the lovely hills and the great stretches of water that lie between them. If I had not already seen the Lakes, I would have been forced to take them on trust.

But, even so, it was difficult to believe that beyond the immediate blanket of fine drizzle the hills were rising in green grandeur towards the sky.

I pulled up at the lakeside at Windermere and lunched in a hotel full of storm-bound people. They sat gloomily eating, with their eyes on the lake and on the water falling on the lake, pricking its dark surface with millions of pin-point splashes; and they seemed to have lost all initiative.

As a matter of fact a wet day in the Lakes can be the most stimulating experience if you walk and climb and enjoy the rain on your face and the rain on your clothes. If I were a doctor I would prescribe wet weather in the Lakes for a variety of complaints, from over-eating, which is one of the most common diseases of this age, to melancholia, which is another.

The population of Lakeland may be divided into two groups – those who stay on the water level, sail in boats, seek suicide in their cars on the narrow roads and drink coffee after dinner on neat lawns at the lake-side; and those who, rising early, put on shorts, grasp stout sticks and leave the ground level before the first group have had their morning tea.

These picturesque ones are, to my mind, the only people who get the true value from the Lakes. Had I more time I would join them, for the only way to enjoy this country is to climb away from the

Derwent Water

crowds and seek solitude in the bosky silence of woods or on the craggy heights of fells. I like to see the real Lakelanders returning covered in dust and victory as the shades of night are falling fast.

I will not dare to compare the soft beauty of Windermere with the majesty of Derwentwater or the grand solitude of Ullswater, or the high serenity of Thirlmere and Coniston. If I have any preference it is for the smallest of them all: little Rydal Water, which is three-quarters of a mile long and, beside these watery giants, is just a spoonful of blue in a cup of green hills. Rydal Water is a magic, satisfying lakelet – a little looking-glass in which the woody heights, by which it is hemmed, lie as in a mirror.

I saw it first at night. It was a clear, moonlit night, with no breath of wind among the trees. In the middle of the little lake, round and golden as a guinea, lay the moon. Sights such as this, hiding round a corner, lurking behind trees and suddenly revealed, pull a man up sharply and fling him on his knees. Had Rydal Water been in Cornwall or in Wales nothing could have disconnected it from the Excalibur legend; and most men would have believed it, for this is a mystic mere . . .

Rydal Water from Dora's Field

C ARLISLE CASTLE was for centuries the chief bulwark in the north-west against our friend the Scot. For centuries the claymores whistled round it; for centuries the sentries, watching through the narrow slits in the Norman keep, strained their eyes for a movement from the Cheviots and their ears for that incredibly eerie sound, a skirl of pipes over the hills.

You can see a small semi-underground dungeon in which, in 1745, three hundred captured Scotsmen were packed tight so that they fought together in the foul darkness to reach the air from the narrow window slits. When the gaolers went to this 'Black Hole of Carlisle' in the morning the dead lay trampled to death beneath the bodies of those who still lived.

More dramatic, more horrible even than this story, because you can see it and feel it, is a stone low down in the wall of another dungeon. This underground cell has never known daylight. The prisoners had to mount a narrow ledge some few feet above the level of the floor. There they were manacled and chained by the neck so that if they stepped from the ledge they hanged themselves; a release which I suppose many of them welcomed. At certain times they were unchained in order that they might walk about. They discovered in this fetid dungeon a stone which was colder than the rest. They must have felt it in the dark. It is still ice-cold. No one knows the reason for this. It seems to sweat frozen moisture. And this stone – I have seen nothing more terrible in any torture chamber – is hollowed out

102

Carlisle Castle

by the fevered tongues of the men once imprisoned in this vile hole. Just above it, cut inches deep in a higher stone, is the shape of a hand worn in the stone by the fingers of hundreds – thousands – of poor wretches as they bent down to place their parched tongues to the licking stone.

High up in the keep of Carlisle Castle they imprisoned Macdonald of Keppoch, who was captured during the Scottish rising of 1745. His little window looked out to Scotland; and the red sandstone is worn an inch deep to the shape of his fingers as he stood there month after month gazing hungrily towards the Cheviot Hills. Is there a more pitiful relic of the struggle between England and Scotland?

Macdonald covered the walls of his prison with the most remarkable carvings, executed, so they say, with a nail. There is nothing so elaborate in the state cells of the Tower of London. Notable among his carving is the figure of a naked woman with enormous hips. She recurs frequently in his painstaking designs. She could be sold at Sotheby's as a good example of primitive Egyptian art.

This castle is the abiding memory of Carlisle.

104

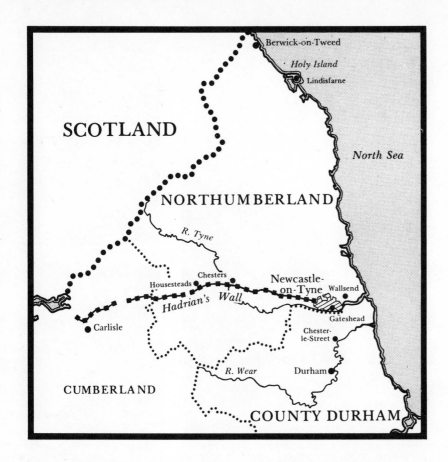

C OULD I MAKE A BARGAIN with Time I would roll back seventeen centuries so that I might meet any Roman centurion who
served on the Wall of Hadrian during the three hundred years of its
military occupation. I would shake him warmly by the hand, stand
him a drink, and say:

'I'm sorry, Marcus! I sympathise with you! I crossed the Wall
from Carlisle – which you called Luguvallium – to Newcastle-on-
Tyne – which you knew as Pons Aelii – and it rained, Marcus – how
it rained! Seventy-three miles of rain over the Wall, and, by Jupiter,
such rain!'

He would, I am sure, look interested.

'It still comes down like Hades, does it?' he would ask. 'Fancy
that! We thought it was organised by the local gods against the
Empire. It used to put out the cook-house fires, get into the wine-
skins, give the Spanish cavalry frog, and when you stood on the
parapet it would beat up against your face, blinding you and,
oozing behind your chin strap, make your face smart like blazes.
Jove's bolts! What a Wall!'

That rain from Carlisle to Newcastle! It swooped down from the north in great blown sheets, and it swept up from the south and met the northern sheets in mid-air above the wall, there they fought in cross currents and fell together, lashing the earth. Every few miles I left the car by the wayside and plodded off over soggy fields to spot the wall, which you can trace almost without a break for seventy-three miles.

At Housesteads I stood thrilled to the marrow. I have seen Pompeii, and I have seen Timgad in Africa, but to see this great Roman monument in our own cold northern lands! That wall was the north boundary wall of the Roman Empire.

Yew Tree Farm,
Coniston

TOP LEFT Chesters
LEFT Footbath
at Chesters

Hadrian's Wall, near Housesteads

I stood wet through in Chesters and went over the ruins of one of the largest forts on the Wall: Cilurnum it was called when the second ala of Asturian cavalry were stationed there.

How little imagination it takes to see this Wall as it was: an eighteen-foot barrier from sea to sea, a tower or pill-box every mile and, dotted along the length, stone fortresses garrisoned by cohorts and alas. And behind each fort grew up villages where the married quarters were: villages with shops and workshops, and temples.

It is strange to think that for three hundred years the nations of Europe formed a defensive crust along the north of England. The Regular Army was at York and Chester, but the Wall was in the hands of the territorials, or auxiliary legions recruited wherever Rome had made conquests. Here, in the blinding rain and in the winter snows, were shivering Moors from Africa, men from Spain, from the forests of Germany, of France, of Belgium. All Europe and parts of Africa helped to defend England for three hundred years.

No doubt in time these foreign legions were alien in name only. When drafts did not come from distant lands I imagine that the villages behind the forts gave many half-British recruits to the Eagles.

WHAT A BLACK PRINCE OF A CITY! Newcastle stands on its hill like a knight in sable armour. The first impression is one of strength. It looks as though it should make battleships and armour plate.

The view across the river where the immense high-level bridge flings its line so lightly over the Tyne is, I think, the most impressive sight of its kind in the north of England. If I were a painter I could never weary of this bridge. It has as many moods as a woman. I would like to paint it in the early morning when it stretches into a faint pearly mist from which rise up the vague silhouettes of roofs, chimney-pots and spires. It is different again in the evening when a rust-red sunset smoulders over Newcastle; it is, perhaps, most wonderful on a night of stars with a railway train going over it.

Here, or hereabouts, stood Hadrian's Bridge which carried the legions westward along the wall. It would be good to paint it with the ghost of the Roman bridge near it, so much lower in the water; a railway train on the modern bridge and a grey cohort of Roman cavalry crossing the old bridge, their plumes blowing in the wind. That, too, would express Newcastle-on-Tyne: it is a queer, romantic mix-up of English history. The best Wallsend coal preserves the name of the terminal station on the Roman Wall; Gateshead owes its name to the bridge of Hadrian.

I wonder how many natives of Newcastle have been inside the Castle Keep. It is one of the most magnificent pieces of late Norman

Tyne Bridges

architecture in England. In its very depths is a little chapel as complete and perfect as the Norman chapel in the Tower of London.

I RAN INTO BERWICK-ON-TWEED in the evening. Berwick has been tossed about for centuries between the Scots and the English. It now belongs officially to England, but the speech of the natives suggests that it still belongs to Scotland!

It is a hilly little stone town built where the Tweed pours itself into the sea. It has an embattled air. Parts of it look as though the Scots (or the English) had just raided it. It still has the appearance of a frontier fortress.

The little island of Lindisfarne, called Holy Island, lies off the Northumbrian coast some three miles south of Berwick. When the sun shines its sands light up, so that Lindisfarne, seen from the mainland, looks like a gold ship anchored at sea. At high tide the island is cut off from England, but when the tide is low you can approach it over three miles of watery and slippery sands.

Bridge at Berwick

OPPOSITE
Northumberland

The wide sands, pricked for miles with millions of worm moulds, reflected the gold clouds and were alive with eager, noisy, or industrious sea birds – gulls, oyster-catchers, kittiwakes, sandpipers – flying in white clouds or standing in pools of sea-water. A line of posts marched over the sands towards Lindisfarne marking the way.

Holy Island! It is one of the sacred places of England. Thirteen centuries ago, when the north was a heathen land, the Celtic hermits from Iona chose Lindisfarne as the place to make their cells because it looked a wild, unhappy place, in which the flesh might be utterly subdued. (It still looks like that.) They made of it a little Thebaid in cold British waters. It became not Lindisfarne, but Holy Island. A Saxon king sent his officers to kneel on the sands of Lindisfarne and hold a crozier towards St Cuthbert, as they begged this holy man to become bishop. In this lovely April of Christianity miracles took place on the island and from that little bare rock in the sea the Love of Christ went out to conquer the North of England.

Time has done little to Holy Island. It is a lovely solitude. It is ringed about with the cry of gulls and the thunder of the sea.

'*A line of posts marched over the sands towards Lindisfarne marking the way.*'

Statue of St Aidan,
Lindisfarne Priory

The Harbour

A few hundred fisher-folk live in small stone houses. The men are brawny with brick-red faces, the women tall and muscular and, some of them, extraordinarily handsome and graceful. They are like members of one family. Their unusual cordiality marks them off from other isolated peoples, and there is, I am assured, no vice of any kind in Holy Island; which is, of course, right.

I AM WRITING beside the River Wear, surrounded by flies, small winged dragons, and minute centipedes, which paddle drearily through the ink before route-marching all over the paper. It is a beautiful day. I went, with passionate sincerity, to do nothing except lie back and continue to look at one of the finest sights in Europe.

High on a red sandstone hill, lifted like a challenge above the heads of the tallest trees, stands Durham Castle. Behind the battle-mented walls, which are built sheer on the cliff's edge, rise the lovely, red-brown towers of Durham's Norman cathedral. Durham Castle crowns its hill like an armoured knight, and the city of Durham crowds round Durham Hill – a tight mass of houses and a main street no wider than a country lane – clustering round the fortified height as serfs might cling to the baron's keep for protection. Durham is in appearance as feudal as His Majesty's Tower of London.

What a site for a castle and a church. To sit beside this wide, slow river and to look up at this hill is to see Norman England. How much romance, beauty and drama can be skipped over by a guide book! As I was standing behind the high altar of Durham Cathedral earlier in the day I saw a large platform with one word carved on the stone: 'Cuthbertus'. The guide book says: 'In the place of honour behind the high altar is the tomb of St Cuthbert, who died AD 687. The body still rests below . . .'

When St Cuthbert died in the Holy Isle of Lindisfarne he told his monks that if the pirates came again they must promise to bear his his body with them wherever they might go. In 870 the long boats of the Danes were beached on the north-east coast, and the monks of Lindisfarne, faithful to their word, took flight, carrying with them the body of St Cuthbert, and in the same coffin the head of St Oswald. They journeyed through South Scotland and North England where the many old churches dedicated to St Cuthbert mark, no doubt, their resting-places. After eight years' wandering they settled near Durham at Chester-le-Street. Here for over one hundred years the body of the saint was undisturbed.

Then the Danes came again! Once more the faithful monks bore their coffin away, and finally in 995 they came to the high red cliff at Durham, and there they built over the sacred body a little wattle church. They built a wooden church and then a stone one. Into this

Northumberland, near Asholm

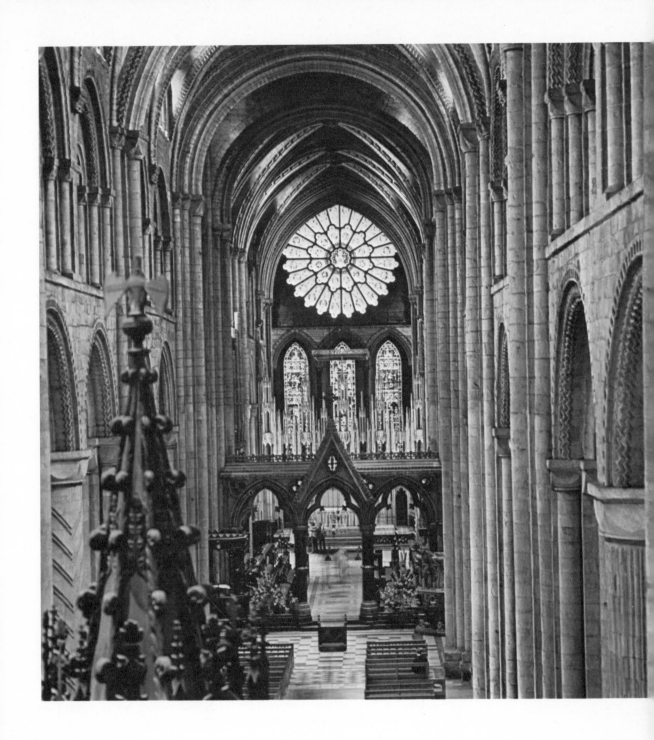

LEFT Durham from the Wear
ABOVE The cathedral nave

stone church it is said King Canute walked barefoot to the shrine of St Cuthbert . . .

In 1069, three years after the Conquest, William sent a Norman follower to be Earl of Northumbria. The men of Durham promptly slew him and his troops. This led to that appalling reign of terror in the north of England. William and his cavalry went through the north like a cyclone. They systematically stamped out life between Durham and York. They left behind them a country of charred ruins.

After this cruel display of authority Durham Cathedral rose up on its hill under Norman chisels. Its great nave, upheld by giant stone columns, was built by the notorious Flambard. It is, with the exception of the hypostyle hall in the great temple of Karnak in Egypt, the most awe-inspiring temple I have seen. It seemed to me, as I stood near the west door of Durham and looked at this vast dim church, whose pillars are like giant oaks, whose arches are austere, whose sanctuaries are built as if to withstand a siege, that this building is a declaration of Norman policy. I almost heard the voice of the Conqueror ringing down the nave:

'Look at this church! I have conquered England, and in England I intend to stay. When you pray here remember how I went with fire and sword through the north to punish you. I am very strong!'

That, so it seems to me, is the message of Durham Cathedral. It is a proof in stone of the strong new blood that had come into England.

Few people, I imagine, in proportion to those who visit the Cathedral, ever enter the library. It is an astonishing place. No monastic establishment in England has left remains more complete than Durham, and the library forms a group of buildings second only in interest to the church.

This library is the old dormitory of the monks; at right angles to it and now incorporated with it is a building which in the old days formed the greater and lesser refectories in which the monks took their frugal meals. The first thing you notice are the immense beams which span the roof. The oaks from which they are formed came from the Prior's Woods at Beaurepaire (now Bearpark, about two and a half miles from Durham), and they have stood there for six hundred years.

In a glass case you see the remains of the coffin lid made by the monks of Lindisfarne twelve hundred and eighty years ago. The piece of it that has survived is about five feet long and sixteen inches wide, and on it, crudely carved but with great spirit and sincerity, are pictures of Our Lord and symbols of the four Evangelists. On one end is a drawing of the Virgin Mary with the Infant Jesus, on the other St Gabriel and St Michael. There are also rude impressions of

St Cuthbert's coffin

the twelve Apostles and St Paul, probably also St Barnabas. These pictures have, it seems, been cut with a knife or a chisel.

The visitor who looks on these relics and cannot build up a picture of the early days of Christianity on windy Lindisfarne is to be pitied. These little snuff-brown fragments of wood, light and soft as tinder, were part of that coffin which the monks carried for hundreds of years during the wanderings of St Cuthbert; they formed part of the wooden shrine in which his body was enclosed twelve years after his death.

6 Yorkshire

EVERYONE IN THE SOUTH of England should visit Whitby if only to see how Yorkshire can imitate the best of Devon and Cornwall. Whitby is the Brixham or Polperro of the north-east coast. It also contains artists who reproduce its beauties on the walls of Burlington House, but you would never know this. They do not stand out from the landscape in sackcloth and ringlets as such colonies do in the south.

Two high green cliffs are separated by the valley of the River Esk. The Old Town of Whitby clings to the steep east cliff, its red-tiled houses are like a colony of scarlet mussels clustered on a rock. The roofs are ranged one above the other in irregular terraces, the red tiles and the tall chimneys form one of the prettiest roof-lines in England. High above the Old Town, at the summit of one hundred and ninety-nine stone steps, and almost on the edge of the cliff, is the silver-grey skeleton of the Abbey of Whitby, the abbey of the holy virgin St Hilda, where Caedmon, the cowherd monk, received his famous vision one night as he lay among the oxen. There also, thirteen hundred years ago, took place that first important debate between the Celtic and the Roman Churches; and at that same Synod of Whitby was fixed the still puzzling date of Easter.

On the other side of the gorge is New Whitby, a neat, respectable Kensingtonian series of terraces set about with gardens and close-cut stretches of turf. New Whitby, which is quite uninteresting to me, is, however, the land of promise.

When the sun has gone down you must climb the one hundred and ninety-nine steps and stand in the gaunt shadow of St Hilda's Abbey.

As the light goes out of the sky and the wind drops you will hear, like the voice of the sea, the steady tolling of a bell over the waters. They say that long ago a heathen pirate beached his ship at Whitby and, scaling the cliff with his war band, raided the abbey and carried off the great bells from the tower. No sooner had he made for open sea with his booty than a darkness came over the sky, a wind sprang up from nowhere, and the sea, hitherto calm, becoming of great violence, rose about the pirate galley in such mountainous waves that the ship sank and the bells fell to the bottom of the sea, where they still lie. They say, in addition, that if a lover will go up to the Abbey ruins at midnight on All-Hallows' Eve and, standing face to the sea, will whisper his sweetheart's name he will, should fate be on his side, hear faint and ghostly from beneath the sea the great bells of Whitby ringing a wedding peal . . .

Every still evening you can hear a bell tolling out to sea; and in any other part of England you would admit that it is a bell-buoy.

WHEN YOU ARE IN THIS PART OF THE WORLD wait for a sunny morning with a wind blowing, take a long last look at the bay where the white horses ride, and go inland towards Pickering. You will pass through the little village of Thornton Dale, which is said to be the prettiest village in Yorkshire. (It is not; there is no 'prettiest' village in Yorkshire!)

Now at Pickering the cosy greenness of the Vale of York piles itself up in fat fields and silver orchards, and stops. In these lanes you meet a man and a cow going for a walk together. Sometimes the man is taking the cow, sometimes the cow is taking the man, in which case the man steers it by tapping its brown posterior from time to time with a hedge switch. The newspaper contents bills in these villages seem like an echo from another planet. I am sure that these kindly, smiling people read their Sunday murders as children read Hans Andersen. All this important simplicity ceases at Pickering. North of this little up-and-down town the moors begin. Pickering is a frontier town. Its stone houses huddle together as if banded against the wildness that lies at their very doors. And the road north out of Pickering leads up into the heart of a gold cloud.

The York moors are the Dartmoor of the north of England. Their bare ridges slope against the sky, moor folded against moor in long perspective like enormous frozen billows. The light is never constant. The moving skyscape flings new colours over the moorland as the clouds change pattern against the sun.

Experienced-looking cock pheasants who have earned their old-age pensions explode suddenly from the heather and fly low down across the road; an occasional rabbit cocks his long ears to you; the larks, fluttering motionless high in the air, send down their trembling song; and the gorse flames in patches, mile after mile. The distant ridges are blue as hot-house grapes.

It is a cold, inspiring hardness that looks as if it has never given food or shelter to man or beast. An infrequent tree, its boughs

Yorkshire, the village
of Bramham

124

deformed, leans against the wind, and the brown heather, soggy
with little peaty streams that well up from nowhere and trickle to
nowhere, is alive with the restless breezes.

T HERE ARE MOMENTS when the traveller stops and says to himself: 'My journey has ended almost before it has begun. There is
no point in continuing it. I shall, if I follow the high road for a
hundred years, find nothing more lovely than this.'

Three times have I said these words in one day's wandering as I
stood before the ruined altars of Fountains, Jervaulx, and Rievaulx.
These abbeys are the three glories of the North Riding. There should
be some charitable fund for the transportation of all spiritually
diseased and all unhappy people to these abbeys. Here Peace and
Beauty live hand in hand.

I would say to any man or woman in England who is longing for a
spiritual experience: 'Go to Ripon and visit these three abbeys in
turn.' Their white bones are drenched in peace; all the pride has
gone out of them and they kneel in the Yorkshire meadows with
white daisies about them like three saints at prayer. Strange and
puzzling are the emotions of a Protestant in these abbeys. I cannot
echo George Borrow and rejoice that scenes of gross superstition lie
in ruins; I cannot feel the horror of a Roman Catholic for the
Reformation which brought about their fall, but where is the man
who cannot feel pity for such beauty in distress, where is the man who
cannot feel contempt for the rough, unfeeling hands which tore such
loveliness to the earth?

ABOVE LEFT Sheep on Birkda

126

Levisham Moor

'Below is the silver-grey ruin of Rievaulx Abbey lying snugly cupped in the valley and the moors rise up beyond it rolling to the sky.'

The high altar of Fountains Abbey is covered with a stubborn green moss the colour of olives. In the late afternoon the sunlight slants over the western walls and, falling into the roofless church, prints sharp gold squares and triangles on the Norman columns of the nave. Small birds fly through the clerestory windows, and the brightest and softest patch of turf in all England lies like a soft carpet from the high altar to the great west door. When you look through the windows, in which not one inch of glass remains, you may fancy that the green leaves and the interlaced boughs beyond form themselves into sacred patterns against the gaping frames.

It is so quiet. I sit writing near the high altar, which stands raised above the body of the church, a large desolate slab of stone. I remember the Frenchman who said to Richard I:

'You have at home in England three daughters whom you love

LEFT the road to
Gordale Scar
RIGHT Fountains Abbey

more than the grace of God; they are Pride, Luxury, and Avarice.'

'My friend,' replied the King, 'they are no longer at home. I have
married Pride to the Templars, Luxury to the Black Canons, and
Avarice to the Cistercians.'

But there was a time before this marriage when the good monks
wandered the roads of England looking for a place in which to found
their abbeys. I prefer to think of them at their highest rather than at
their lowest; and at their highest they saved for us all that was left of
culture and of knowledge. How did they build these incredibly
beautiful abbeys? I put this question to an architect the other day,
and he made a surprising answer:

'They sang,' he said, 'and their work was done for them.'

They sang! Go to Fountains and remember that; for this church
looks, is indeed, a psalm in stone. They came from York, tramping

Fountains Abbey,
the Cellarium

the wild countryside, poor, humble, hungry, dreaming only of
raising a temple to the glory of God, and they took stone from the
local quarries and carried it to the thorny meadow by the stream and
– they sang! So the great Abbey of Fountains rose up from the grass, a
reflection of their magnificent faith!

The sun was setting as I left Fountains and took the road through
Ripon and then north-west to West Tanfield and Masham. Here the
green valley fades imperceptibly into the harder moors and fells of
the Pennine Chain. Away to the right I saw the Abbey of Jervaulx
lying in a meadow some little distance from the road.

This great tangled ruin was like something on the other side of
fairyland, it was like the Palace of the Sleeping Beauty.

I sat in the chapter-house in a monk's stall over which brambles
and small blue rock-flowers had formed a close embroidery. Six
pillars which once upheld the roof pointed to the sky, their feet in
ivy. On the floor lay the gravestones of mitred abbots. And I remembered the lovely story of this abbey, a fresh, beautiful story full
of the early morning of the world, how a company of monks from
the parent abbey of Byland were lost among these moors and fields
and how as they slept the abbot was given a vision. A woman and
her little boy appeared to him.

132

'Fair and tender woman,' he said to her, 'what doest thou with thy child in this barren and deserted place?'

She smiled with her eyes before replying:

'I am a frequent inmate of desert places. I have come from Rievaulx and Byland and am going to the new monastery.'

Then the abbot, who was relieved to have found a guide in the wilderness, said:

'Good lady, I implore thee to lead me and my brethren to the new monastery, for we also are of Byland.'

She then said, with the same slow smile:

'Ye were of Byland but are now of Jervaulx.'

Turning to her little boy she said:

'Sweet son, be their leader, I am called elsewhere.'

And she disappeared.

The boy led the way, holding a branch pulled from a tree, and the monks followed him until they came to a barren, desolate place among the hills. Here the child thrust the branch into the earth and immediately it became filled with white birds. He looked at the monks, saying: 'Here shall God be adored for a short space,' and before they, having recognised Him, could fall on their knees in the grass He also vanished . . .

'Here shall God be adored for a short space.'

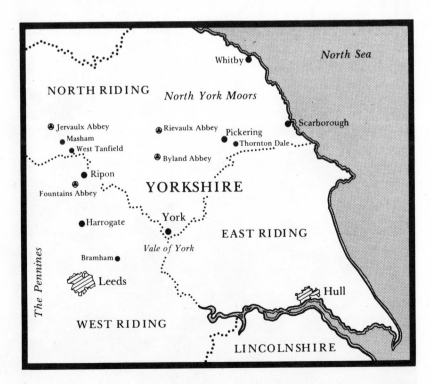

*'In full noon sunshine
you would not be
surprised to meet
a sheik in a blue
burnous riding a white
Barbary stallion up
one of Scarborough's
many hilly streets.'*

IT WAS EARLY IN THE EVENING. The sun was going down over the Vale of York and the grey towers of the Cathedral Church of St Peter rose over the flat lands. There was a wind blowing at my back or I might have heard the minster bells, whose chimes, on a still evening, go over the fields for miles. As I went on between the hedges my spirits rose, because York is the loveliest city in all England. She is England's last real anchor to the Middle Ages. Other cities have cathedrals, one has a wall, many have castles and ancient houses, but York is the supreme, unselfconscious queen of them all. She does not ask you to love her: she is like London in that. She is there: she is York.

York, let me tell you, is the last city in England which a man should enter on horseback or on foot. Unfortunately few people know this! When I came to the high, white, machicolated wall that circles the city I looked up at the great bastions that guard its angles, at the cross-slits for the bowmen, at the gate-houses on whose topmost turrets little stone men, outlined against the sky, hug boulders to their stomachs and seem about to heave them down on you as you pass.

The street names of York are so eloquent that no words of mine can better describe the flavour of this ancient city. Listen to them: Gillygate, Fossgate, Shambles, Spurriergate, Goodramgate, Coppergate, Swinegate, Ogle Forth, Tanners' Moat, Palmers' Lane, Aldwark . . .

The walls of York lift you above the chimney pots. On one side is a six-foot fortification pierced every few yards with square, waist-high openings for boiling oil or for archers. Through these openings you look down over the green moat to the back gardens and the homes of York outside the wall where, in the early morning, people are

College Street, York

The Shambles

awakening, pulling up blinds, making tea, dressing the babies – a peaceful scene which would have astonished the fifteenth-century sentinels more than an army with banners!

How strange they would have thought it to hear on that spot, where in winter the wolves bayed Bootham Bar, no sound more painful than some Yorkist in the throes of teething!

On the other side the ground falls away from the wall to the cathedral and the deanery gardens. You see York Minster through a hedge of silver-white blossom. Everything is silver-white in the early sun. The wall itself is silver-white. Tadcaster stone is washed by every rain, so that the Wall of York has always looked new. And this white, enchanted ribbon twists on and round, never straight for more than twenty yards, losing itself in green bowers as the tops of the trees on either side arch themselves over the white bastions.

136

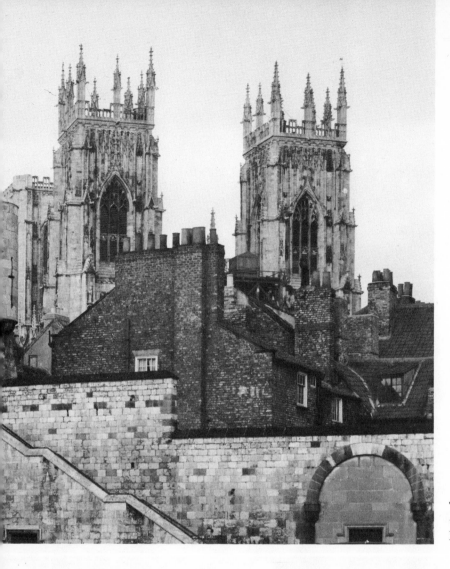

The Walls and
the Minster from
Bootham Bar

The glory of York Minster is the glory of its glass. It is said to con-
tain two-thirds of the fourteenth-century glass in England. The 'Five
Sisters' window is a queen among windows, a tall, slender, mellow
poem in glass for which I have no words. No words can describe it:
it must be seen.

In the crypt of the minster, hidden away in the dark, is a well. This
well lay there before the great cathedral was built; the cathedral
was, in fact, built to cover this well. The first cathedral of York was a
wooden chapel erected over this well for the baptism on Easter Day,
AD 627, of King Edwin of Northumbria and all his court.

The face of the minster is washed by a pink flush from the west. In
a few moments the quiet dusk will be stealing through the streets of
York and 'Great Peter' will solemnly tick another hour from the
slate of eternity.

SHIPS SAIL RIGHT INTO THE HEART of Hull. They saunter casually across the main streets, their masts become mixed up with the electric cable poles. Trawlers steam in from the North Sea across roads and nestle their smoke stacks against the chimneys of Hull. Barges roll in casually, with the skipper smoking his pipe and looking up pleasantly at the long line of taxis, oil-cake lorries, cement mixers and buses which wait respectfully for the bridge to swing back.

It is not perhaps remarkable that Hull is one of England's mis-understood cities. There are many reasons for this. She lies, like

Hull Docks

Norwich, in a big geographical bulge, rather off the track from the ordinary travellers' point of view, so that few people arrive there by mistake and discover her. Her name is short, sharp and snappy. It sounds modern and cocksure. It is a name with a cigar in the corner of its mouth and a Stetson on its head. Worst of all, the most famous remark about Hull compares her to Hell!

All this is most unfair. The first thing you learn in Hull is that this monosyllable is not her real name, it is merely her telegraphic address. Her real name is the King's Town upon the Hull, or, as they write it on buses and official documents, Kingston-upon-Hull. That gives, to me at least, an entirely new conception of the place. The king whose town this is was Edward I – Longshanks – who must have had a good eye as well as a good leg, because he made Hull a seaport in the thirteenth century. No other port in England was deliberately selected as such by an English king.

You respect the Humber fisherman when you remember that it is from the old whaling stock that he comes. When you see him in the fish market landing his catch, you think of the bigger fish his fathers caught. You remember the queer old prints in the museum which show him iced up in the Arctic, great bergs towering above the ships. He amused himself at such moments by cruising through the broken ice in small boats, taking a pot shot at a walrus or trying to catch a diffident polar bear. Now the men of the Humber, living in a world which fortunately needs no corsets and no whalebone, go out after the haddock.

I spent an exciting hour among the relics of Hull's whaling days. How lucky is Hull in her museums! The Museum of Fisheries and Shipping – which sounds as dull as the Ministry of Agriculture – is packed with the thrilling relics of these times: the harpoons, the walrus skulls, the tusks, the queer curios which the whalers brought back with them; the carved ships and the rude paintings made by them during their long vigil in the polar seas.

In one of Hull's ubiquitous museums is an amusing collection of motor cars. It becomes more interesting and valuable as time goes on. It traces the development of the car from the first incredible 'stink-cart', designed like a brougham, down to the comparatively recent but now quite comic motor cars which our grandfathers drove. Few things are more calculated to fill us with reverence for the bravery of our grandfathers than these queer machines.

7 Lincolnshire and East Anglia

CITIES HAVE AS MANY MOODS AS MEN, or I might add with reverence, women.

Some cities hide behind hills and show themselves to the traveller on the high road only at the last moment, as if unwilling to be discovered. Other cities prefer to surprise you: they spring out at you from an apparently innocent landscape, while a few – and these are perhaps rare – stand up nakedly against the white sky and call to you from far off. Lincoln is one of these.

The city of Lincoln is an inland St Michael's Mount. The flat, level fenlands stretch to the sky like a green and yellow sea – an ocean of grass and wheat. On clear days the towers of Lincoln Cathedral are visible for thirty miles, and the view of Lincoln on its hill, lying sharply cut against the distant horizon at the end of a Roman road, is one of the characteristic sights of England. It typifies Fenland, it is one of those quick-change landscape acts for which England is so famous – a sign that you have left the north and have entered the flat lands of the east.

When I ran through Kirton in Lindsey, I saw Ermine Street running ahead for over sixteen miles, like a straight tape. At the end of the road, so small and clear, was Lincoln Hill. Every minute, almost with every second, the towers of the cathedral grew larger at the end of the road, till, at the last mile or so, they filled the sky. And I sang the legions' marching song about Lalage and Rimini . . .

Lincoln lies on two levels. Old Lincoln on the hill has its feet in the past; new Lincoln below the hill made the tanks during the war.

One of the most interesting relics in Old Lincoln is the Newport Arch, the only Roman town gate still in use in England. I stood before this massive grey gate and watched motor cars run in under the arch which has admitted the spears of the legions into Lindum. This arch has a little side arch, or 'Needle's Eye'. I believe many people think of the camel and the eye of the needle quite literally; if so, the

Lincoln Cathedral

Newport Arch makes this Bibical reference plain. The town gates in the east were shut at dusk, but the Needle's Eye was open. A caravan arriving after the gates were shut had to camp outside the walls, but the master of the caravan could pass in through the small gate – a physical impossibility to his camels – and seek lodgings in the city . . .

On the level Lincoln is alive with crowds at night, but as you mount the steep hill, holding on to the hand rail which is there to assist you, you mount up to quiet and peace. Between the eaves of old houses you see the massive screen of the west front and the twin towers of the great church lifted against the stars. You can think of Rome, if you like, or of the last journey from Lincoln of the dead queen, Eleanor, which ended at the Cross at Charing: or you can think of nothing but the gracious beauty that lives in these stones.

A MAN WHO LOVES the rounded contour of the West Country is at first inclined to dislike the flat monotony of the Lincolnshire Fens. His eye looks round vainly for landmarks; there is nothing on which to focus. The flat land runs to the sky on all sides, and the presence of the sea is over the moving corn. Gradually, however, the peculiar atmosphere of the country grips the imagination. The slightest eminence becomes important; a windmill or a tall tree occupies the eyes, and the flight of birds is marvellous against the sky. As in all flat countries, the clouds billow splendidly over the rim of the earth, and you find the greatest beauty in the changing heavens.

The third 'part' or 'riding' of Lincolnshire is called Holland, and no district in England has been more justly named. I was heading for Holland when, standing up about ten miles away, I saw a curious tower among the fields.

'That's Boston Stump!' said a man in a cornfield.

'And what is Boston Stump?' I asked.

'It's Boston Stump!' he replied, and added 'Thickhead' with his eyes.

So, feeling there was no point in provoking him further, I slid off along the level way.

Boston in Holland . . .

As I drew near, the Stump proved to be the tower of a fine old Dutch church, standing on the brink of a slow, canal-like river. In a few moments I entered the cobbled streets of a town which, like Bradford-on-Avon in Wiltshire, bears the stamp of the foreign trader.

Boston today is an interesting study. It is typical of the great town that has come down in the world. Like many an aristocrat, it manages to carry on bravely, so that, unless you knew of its past grandeur, there would be nothing remarkable about its present condition. In

Boston Stump

the Middle Ages Boston was the Bristol of the East Coast. There was no greater port in England, except London. The decline began with the Black Death, which decimated the eastern counties. The sea broke through the dikes, Boston Harbour wilted, and the final blow was delivered by the gradual shifting of the commercial balance from east to west coast with the development of trade with the Americas. Boston at this time contributed to the very cause of her eclipse; her men helped to found Boston, New England, and now, by one of those queer tricks of time, the citizens of the famous Boston (Mass.) roam the quiet streets of the little-known English Boston commenting on its quaintness.

Norfolk fisherman

I WAS LOST IN A NORFOLK LANE, so I stopped a man and I said to him:

'Good morning!'

He looked at me.

'Good morning,' I cried. 'Can you tell me if I am right for Norwich?'

He continued to look at me. Then, in an uneasy, suspicious way, he said: 'What d'ye want to know for?'

I might have been annoyed, but leaning out of the car and putting on an affable expression which I usually keep for tea-parties, I said:

'My dear old 'bor, I want to know because I want to get to Norwich.'

The ghost of a smile flitted over his rustic face, and he replied after some deep thought, rather reluctantly, and looking away from me:

'Well, you're right!'

I don't expect anyone to believe this unless he knows Norfolk.

Norfolk is the most suspicious county in England. In Devon and Somerset men hit you on the back cordially; in Norfolk they look as though they would like to hit you over the head – till they size you up. You see, for centuries the north folk of East Anglia were accustomed to meet stray Vikings on lonely roads who had just waded ashore from the long boats.

'Good morning, 'bor!' said the Vikings. 'Which is the way to the church?'

Norwich, Elm Hill

'What d'ye want to know for?' was the Norfolk retort.

'Well, we thought about setting fire to it!'

You will gather that Norfolk's suspicion of strangers, which is an ancient complex bitten into the East Anglian through centuries of bitter experience, is well grounded, and should never annoy the traveller. They mean well. Once they bring themselves to call you 'bor (which, I conclude, is the short for 'neighbour' or perhaps 'boy'), you can consider yourself highly complimented. In East Anglia men are either neighbours or Vikings. If they promote you to 'bordom they will do any mortal thing for you except, perhaps, lend you money, for one Norfolk farmer could beat any three Yorkshiremen at driving a bargain.

THE MOST SURPRISING THING about Norwich is that it contains the only Norman cathedral in England unknown to Americans. Norwich is not on the pilgrimage map, and the reason is geographical. The tourist stream flows due south from Lincoln to Peterborough – Ely – Cambridge, leaving Norwich in the great eastward bulge of Norfolk fifty miles to the left. Some day, of course, the people who map tours will discover Norwich and some day, maybe, Norwich may even discover itself.

Norwich is a confusing, characteristic city. It was tied up into hasty knots centuries ago and has never been unwound. It is characteristic of Norfolk. It is a monument to the north folk and it bears the marks of all their peculiarities – it has flint walls and is difficult to know at a glance! Norwich in Somerset would be unthinkable; it is an expression of sturdy East Anglia. I came here knowing nothing about the city except that it has always made money, that it once

Norwich Cathedral,
the cloisters

was the third city in England, that when its weaving trade went north after the coalfields, Norwich just put on a flinty face and learned how to make women's shoes. Trust Norwich to survive!

I saw a red-roofed city dominated by two landmarks: a slim cathedral spire second only to Salisbury and a great square Norman castle on a hill in the heart of which – so George Borrow said confidently – sits an old heathen king 'with his sword in his hand and his gold and silver treasures about him'. I went through queer medieval streets, one paved with cobble stones, all distinctively picturesque; some Flemish in appearance, full of houses with the big inverted V on the top storey, where the hand-looms were housed; and at night beside the river I might have been in the England or the Netherlands of the fourteenth century with the moon falling on huddled roofs, the lamplight moving in slow waters, the dark figures of men and women going through dark alley-ways between the leaning eaves.

Strangers' Hall, which stands in a small courtyard in a busy street, is one of the most beautiful small medieval houses you will see in England. Norwich is packed with these unexpected places.

The cathedral is full of splendid Norman work, notably the nave. I imagine that this is the least-known cathedral in England. The clerestory, set back within a wall-passage, has Norman lights; the aisles also are Norman. There is a curious opening in the roof through which the monks used to let down a swinging censer. Norwich Cathedral has not the situation or the west front of Lincoln, but to me it was vastly more interesting than the more famous church.

Beyond Cromer, from Cley-next-the-Sea – which Norfolk men pronounce Cly – the level salt marshes run for miles towards a thin ridge of yellow sand, beyond which is the ocean. The tide goes out for miles and returns at a canter. It is desolate. The wind whispers. The sea birds cry. No men but naturalists disturb the solitude of the salt marshes.

The wind blows through miles of sea lavender, great lakes of pink and purple, and the gold clouds pile up over the edge of the sea and roll landwards like great galleons. The light, falling on this flat land squarely, intensifies colour so that you cry out at sudden glories in the painful knowledge that nothing but water-colour can tell the story truly. The sea marshes are full of life. A blue-grey heron lifts noiselessly above the green reeds and sails away with a slow beat of great wings, his long legs held stiff behind him. He settles. With keen eyes you can see his head lifted to the level of the reeds watching you. White gulls sit in rows on the shells of wrecked fishing boats.

The tide is coming in, rushing in, swirling in up creeks and the twisty channels. One minute the oozy banks are dry; the next they are

ABOVE Blakeney
RIGHT Cley windmill

alive with a brown snake of water that writhes and bubbles, lapping the bright fringe of samphire at the edges.

All along the coast at the edge of the great salt marsh are curious little villages which were once seaports. Huge flint churches in desolate meadows tell you that yesterday this coast was alive with men and commerce. There is Blakeney, whose church has an extra tower, once a lighthouse, now eloquently ruined; there is Cley; there is Salthouse; there is Weybourne, in whose ancient bay the wildfowl nest; there is Wells-next-the-Sea – all old seaports which the sea has deserted.

THE SILENCE OF DEATH lies over the Peddars Way.

A man can walk for many a mile in solitude on this ghost of a mighty road. From Thetford it runs six miles to Hoxham, then, straight as an arrow, it lies for thirty miles, sometimes hidden beneath the fields, through Castle Acre and Great Bircham to the coast at Brancaster. Long before men knew the name of England they knew the Peddars Way. How old it is no man can say. When the Romans came it was an antiquity, trodden hard by countless generations and the Romans were glad, because it was straight and to the point, and saved them trouble. In the Middle Ages the Peddars Way served a new England, and led to one of the saintliest spots in the land – to Our Lady of Walsingham . . .

In that remarkable collection of old houses called Walsingham, north of Fakenham, stands the scanty ruin of the mighty abbey which from the time of Henry III to the Dissolution drew king, queen, and commoner to the shrine of the Virgin. At first the shrine was a modest wooden chapel, but when Nazareth fell into the hands of the infidel the monks of Walsingham, by one of those perhaps not accidental strokes of fancy, for the fortunes of Glastonbury were once firmly financed by another such inspiration, said that the Mother of God, driven out of Palestine, had taken up her abode in Norfolk. They said subsequently that their shrine of Our Lady of Walsingham was actually the Sancta Casa from Nazareth.

Then the Peddars Way became the pilgrims' way. It heard the tapping of the pilgrim staff. It saw men and women from every part of Europe making their way to Walsingham. It saw pilgrim caval-cades like that which Chaucer took so gloriously to Canterbury, it saw the poor man hobbling by the roadside, it saw the King in all his majesty riding a tall charger surrounded by his Court. Henry III, Edward I, Edward II, Bruce of Scotland, Henry VII, and, before the religious revolution, Henry VIII, all took the pilgrims' way to Walsingham.

There came a day when the last pilgrim abased himself before the shrine, and soon the Peddars Way saw men come riding, and in the midst of them Our Lady of Walsingham, plucked from her candle-light, going on her way to be burned at Smithfield. Then the Peddars Way knew that some strange thing had happened to England; and the grass began to grow.

Now the Peddars Way is dead.

I TRAVELLED TOWARDS ELY in the early morning long before the first harvester was awake. At this time of year a veil of white mist lies over the Cambridgeshire fenlands, a pearl pale thing, thin and chill; and as I went on through it I felt as though I were sailing on

Walsingham Abbey from the main gate

The Hundred Foot
Drain

the ghost of a sea. The dimly seen hedges of this flat chessboard land
were like the edges of poised breakers. Suddenly I saw before me, like
a frozen ship upon a frozen ocean, the Isle of Ely rising in spectral
beauty above the morning mist. This sudden high hill crowned with
its towered cathedral seen above the white mist of late summer is one
of the most beautiful things in the whole of England. It is a spellbound
hill: the creation, it seems, of a wizard's wand: a floating Camelot
spun by the fairies from the mushroom mists and ready to dissolve into the cold air even as a man looks in wonder at it.

154

As the sun rises and the mists melt, the Isle of Ely – the Isle of Eels is the real name – grows to reality, becomes a little town on a hill clustered round its old cathedral; but even in full sunlight it never quite loses its air of having been built by magic.

Ely Cathedral, I must remind you, was founded by a woman. It was to this windy island that the saintly Etheldreda in the age of saints took refuge one thousand three hundred and fifty-three years ago. After twelve years of unhappy married life as Queen of Northumbria she fled to her native fens and founded a church, living there

Ely across the floods
RIGHT The lantern
of Ely Cathedral

in great humility and godliness. Memory of her is preserved in the word 'tawdry'. Her popular name was St Audrey, and the famous Pilgrims' Fair at Ely known as St Audrey's Fair gathered together a number of cheap-jacks and hucksters who sold neckcloths of silk nicknamed St Audrey's Chains or, vulgarly, 'tawdries'.

I must mention the monk, Alan of Walsingham, who built the octagonal tower and many other parts of this lovely church. He was one of the greatest architects of the Middle Ages. On 22 February, 1322, just as the monks were retiring to their cells, the old Norman tower of Ely fell down into the choir 'with such a shock', says the old chronicler, 'that it was thought an earthquake had taken place'. Alan of Walsingham 'rose up by night and came and stood over the heap of ruins not knowing whither to turn. But recovering

his courage, and confident in the help of God and of His kind Mother Mary, and in the merits of the holy virgin Etheldreda, he set his hand to the work.'

How magnificently he did so can be seen today. I suppose no one but an architect can truly appreciate the genius of this monk.

I ARRIVED IN COLCHESTER as the sun was setting and decided to stay the night there. In the morning, after visiting the Castle and the Siege House, I took the field-path to Lexden, which overlooks the Colne Valley. Weeks of rain followed by warm spring days had caused the soft earth in the hedge banks to crumble, with the result that large stones were pushed from the soil by their own weight and lay at the foot of the hedge.

As I walked along, prodding the earth here and there with my stick, I was delighted and not too surprised to see a touch of bright red in the brown soil. I placed my stick in the earth slightly above this red streak and flicked out upon the narrow path the base of a Samian bowl with the potter's name neatly inscribed in Roman capitals upon it. The letters I read when I had wiped the caked clay and soil from the potsherd were SEVERUS. F. The F. stands for *fecit*, so the inscription reads: 'Severus made it.'

The well-known Roman potters – and hundreds of them are known with the location of their factories, the dates they exported their various specialities to the most remote corners of the Roman Empire – invariably signed their plates, bowls and vases in this way, or their names in the nominative followed by F. for *fecit*, or their names in the genitive preceded by OF. (*officina*, or workshop), or followed by the letter M. (for *manus*, or 'by the hand of').

Severus was one of the famous East Gaulish potters of the time of Nero. Galley-loads of his bright red wares were shipped to Britain. The shops stocked it in Colonia, which is Colchester; in Londinium; in Verulamium, which is St Albans; in Deva, which is Chester; in Eboracum, which is York. Traders carried it by pack-horse up to the great Wall of Hadrian where we may imagine it decorating the tables of the better sort. Most of this ware was made in Gaul. Severus had his workshop on the Rhine at Neuss, which was then Novaesium, one of the oldest towns in Germany.

In those days Colonia Camulodunum, or Colchester, was more important than the jerry-built trading post on the Thames.

Acknowledgments

For photographic permissions, acknowledgment is made to the following:

Peter Baker : page 49, 50, 128, 129, 136, 143
J. Alan Cash Ltd. : page 8, 12, 30, 38, 60, 62, 65, 87, 93, 128, 138, 144, 146, 150, 154
A. F. Kersting : page 10, 29, 34, 58, 66, 68, 83, 92, 95
Roger Mayne : page 72, 76, 77, 78, 88, 90, 92
Eric Meadows : page 108
Edward Piper : page 82, 112, 113, 116, 125
Kenneth Scowen : page 14, 33, 37, 54, 140
Reece Winstone : page 61
Her Britannic Majesty's Stationery Office: page 108, 109, 132; (with BTA) 114, 131

Royal Commission on Historical Monuments (England): page 80, 156

British Tourist Authority: page 15, 17, 18, 21, 22, 25, 26, 41, 42, 43, 44, 46, 47, 51, 52, 55, 56, 63, 67, 71, 74, 84, 85, 89, 96, 99, 100, 104, 106, 111, 114, 118, 121, 122, 126, 127, 130, 134, 135, 137, 148, 151, 152, 153, 157, endpapers

BTA and Mr G. E. Chantler: Frontispiece; BTA and the Vicar of St Mary's, Warwick: 69; BTA and the National Trust: 103, 107; BTA and the Dean and Chapter of Durham Cathedral: 119; BTA and the Dean and Chapter of Norwich Cathedral: 147

Maps drawn by Jennifer Johnson